THE ART of INVESTMENT

THE ART of INVESTMENT

Third Edition

BARRIE DUNSTAN

The Financial Review Library

A publication of the Financial Review Library,
a publishing division of the John Fairfax Group Pty Ltd ACN 003 357 720

First edition published 1991, reprinted 1991
Second edition published 1992, reprinted 1993
Third edition published 1994

Managing editor: Sarah Hodgkinson
Publishing editor: Ann Atkinson

Printed by McPhersons Printing Group, Victoria
Typeset in Goudy Old Style by DOCUPRO, Sydney

Cover design: Fox Badger Ferret
Indexing: Pam Johnson

Copyright © 1994 in essays Barrie Dunstan
Copyright © 1994 in title and compilations John Fairfax Group Pty Ltd

National Library of Australia
Cataloguing-in-Publication data

Dunstan, Barrie.
  The art of investment.
  3rd ed.

  Includes index.
  ISBN 1 86290 087 6.

  1. Investment-Australia. 2. Stocks-Australia. 1. Title.

332.63220994

CONTENTS

ACKNOWLEDGMENTS

This book emerged only after discussions over a period of time, because initially I believed that there was an over-supply of books on finance and investment. Among those people who changed my mind were Sarah Hodgkinson, the *Australian Financial Review*'s Commercial Business Unit manager, and Chris Lewis of the Australian Stock Exchange bookshop in Melbourne. The emerging shape of the book was influenced also by Peter Griffin of Rothschilds Australia who provided enthusiasm at critical times.

Once the project began, I found many people who willingly helped me with the data, tables and graphs which I have used. I am grateful to Terry Campbell, managing director of J.B. Were & Son, David Peacock of the Australian Stock Exchange research section, Peter Thornhill, marketing director of Perpetual Trustees, and Paul Jenkins, the senior investment manager at Armstrong Jones.

Some of my friends in the investment business also may recognise ideas, views or sayings in this book. Most learning is an amalgam of other people's theories and ideas and I thank all those people over the years who may have added to my knowledge. In my progress through more than three decades of investment writing, I have been fortunate in those who taught me, sometimes unwittingly.

I do, however, want to acknowledge in particular my early mentors in financial journalism: Roy Course of the *Argus* and the *Age*; John Eddy of the *Herald* in Melbourne and John Elsworth of the *Age*. All three were financial journalists who, in their own way, extended the frontiers of the profession. All were consummate professionals and very good teachers, and unfortunately all three died too early to see the extent of the changes in financial journalism which would have excited and even amazed them. This book is dedicated to them.

INTRODUCTION

Surely not another book on investment? That was my first reaction, too. Books on all aspects of investment and finance have proliferated in recent years. Many of them are worthwhile and comprehensive books on how to manage your financial affairs and invest your savings. But most of them, it seemed to me, did two things: they made investment seem very complicated, and they tended to intimidate people.

The Art of Investment, I hope, avoids that. But any book on investment written with a particular viewpoint inevitably will be opinionated and will push the author's point of view or prejudices. So, before you get too far into the book, let me outline my views and put any prejudices on display. Readers can then decide, themselves, what weight to put on any advice.

First, a word about the title, *The Art of Investment*. I do not mean this to elevate investment to a lofty position, but rather to emphasise my view that investment does not necessarily have to be hard work nor the domain of the PhD using quantitative analysis.

For decades in Australia, investment as practised by the major institutional investors was a well-meaning attempt to produce the best returns, sometimes in safety, sometimes not. Then came the measurement of comparative performances. League tables, ranking the best- and worst-performing funds managers, became the way investment managers marketed their services. Suddenly, investment became a game for professionals rather than amateurs.

Subsequently, investment managers discovered modern portfolio theory and the so-called rocket scientists of the 1980s began to apply their quantitative analysis. Today, investment as practised by the professional investors is a complex business, going beyond 'price/earnings ratios' and 'dividend yields' into kingdoms which are bounded by 'efficient frontiers', measured by 'benchmarks' and ruled by 'betas'. The experts now argue that the share market is an 'efficient market' and that a scientific approach based on mathematics and computers can be used to map the investment process.

My background is not scientific. Much of what I learned about investment and the share market was learned at the coalface. That means I have been raised on the fundamental approach to investment, feel more comfortable with shares which offer 'value' rather than 'excitement', and lean towards the contrarian approach—investing contrary to the general market mood or trend.

However, I am fascinated by much of the modern investment theory and the way it has been used to turn investment into a disciplined process. Since the October 1987 stock market collapse when I joined the *Australian Financial Review*, I have increasingly found myself writing about various aspects of investment theory and practice. All this has suggested to me that a systematic approach provides an investment manager with a better chance of producing the best return for investors which, after all, should be the main point of the exercise.

But I do not believe that investment can be turned entirely into a science. Especially for the ordinary person, it is still an art rather than a science, hence the title of this book. I do not intend to denigrate the scientific or quantitative approach to investment. My aim is simply to suggest what I think is the best approach for an individual investor.

The first thing which should be said is that I have assumed that readers who have decided to undertake some investment have some long-term savings put to one side or have a regular savings capacity. The assumption in this book (unless otherwise stated) is that people are investing for periods longer than a couple of years.

This is not a book about how to get rich quick. That requires speculation or gambling. This is about investment, which essentially is about how to get rich, slowly but surely.

In concentrating mostly on the theory of investment, I have left the nuts and bolts of how to go about investing — the money involved and choosing a stockbroker or adviser — mainly to the last part of the book. These are important matters but, in my view, not as important for the average person as understanding that investment is an art which can be practised by most people.

The second thing which should be said it that this book's discussion of investment is skewed towards the stock market. I don't apologise for this; it is simply the area of investment I know best after more than 30 years reporting and writing about the stock market and listed companies. If I had spent 30 years reporting on real estate and property, I might well have written a book with a different emphasis.

There is little point in arguing the merits of one type of equity investment over another. This book argues (and gives the proof in figures) that shares and property are a superior long-term investment to bonds and fixed interest investments. The important thing for investors is to have equities (preferably some of both shares and property) as their all-important long-term investments.

This book is not designed to woo into the stock market those investors who feel more comfortable with real estate or to turn those who have chosen managed investments into direct share investors. As with authors, so investors do best sticking to what they know and understand.

But I would hope that even if readers have a leaning towards real estate or prefer managed products they will approach *The Art of Investment* with an open mind and take the opportunity to discover a different facet of the investment game.

— *Barrie Dunstan*

Almost 60 years ago, the great economist John Maymard Keynes recognised what some people still fail to understand—that the stock market, day to day, had become a large speculative game. He also recognised the ability of those investors able to take a long-term view to make profits.

...the energies and skills of the professional investor and speculator are mainly occupied otherwise. For most of these persons are, in fact, largely concerned not with making superior long-term forecasts of the probable yield of an investment over its whole life but with foreseeing changes in the conventional basis of valuation a short time ahead of the general public. They are concerned not with what an investment is really worth to a man who buys it 'for keeps' but with what the market will value it at, under the influence of mass psychology, three months or a year hence...This battle of wits to anticipate the basis of conventional valuation a few months hence...can be played by the professionals amongst themselves...For it is, so to speak, a game of Snap, of Old Maid, of Musical Chairs...

If the reader interjects that there must surely be large profits to be gained from the other players in the long run by a skilled individual who, unperturbed by the prevailing pastime, continues to purchase investments on the best genuine long-term expectations he can frame, he must be answered, first of all, that there are, indeed, such serious-minded individuals and that it makes a vast difference to an investment market whether or not they predominate in their influence over the game players.

— John Maynard Keynes, 1936

1

INVEST RATHER THAN GAMBLE

It is usually agreed that casinos should, in the public interest, be inaccessible and expensive. And perhaps the same is true of stock exchanges.

— *John Maynard Keynes*

Why should anyone invest money? Perhaps the best reason is the one which most people give when you ask them why they put money into raffles, lotteries or Lotto: You've got to be in it to win it.

These days, however, there are further reasons: the need to establish a fund which will provide income in retirement and the need to hedge against inflation (whether during a working lifetime or in retirement). Both of these are pressing reasons for people to invest their savings, whether by using superannuation, other managed investment schemes or their own initiative.

Since 1 July 1987 there has been an additional incentive for people to invest for themselves — the tax-free nature of ordinary dividends which for many taxpayers provides perhaps the only easy way they can obtain an income which is partly or entirely tax free.

Where companies pay a fully franked dividend (basically, passing on to shareholders the benefit of a rebate of the company tax paid), investors on the maximum marginal tax rate of 48.4 per cent (which includes the Medicare levy) will finish up paying only about 15 to 23 per cent tax, depending on the franking level, on their dividend income. People on lower marginal tax rates will pay

REASONS FOR INVESTING

less and some will pay no tax on their dividends. The rebate from franked dividends also can be used to shelter other income (from wages or salary or from interest on other investments).

Chapter 8 discusses franked dividends in more detail since it is apparent that many investors are ignorant of the imputation system. Results of Australian Stock Exchange (ASX) surveys in 1988 and 1991 showed that a high proportion of shareholders had little or no idea of the tax basis of most of their dividends.

Since the 1987 stock market crash, people have shied away from investing in shares because they regard it as too risky, but these fears appear to be lessening. The 1988 ASX survey found that almost 39 per cent of non-share-owners cited the riskiness of shares as their most important reason for not investing. Three years later, in 1991, the percentage of people worrying about risk declined to just above 28 per cent. A lack of understanding of how the share market works was the next most frequent reason for not investing. Once again, there was an improvement between 1988 and 1991 with the percentage of non-share-owners citing this as a reason for non-investment down from 22 per cent to 20 per cent.

EQUITY INVESTMENTS

Unfortunately, it seems that many people have learned the wrong way how to avoid risk. People avoided equity investments — shares and property — and chased secure investments, usually in capital guaranteed investments which means they are often invested in fixed interest securities. They also have left money on deposit with banks and other institutions. All these investments have their place; indeed for the last few years, investors who left their funds in short-term, near-cash holdings generally outperformed most investment managers' portfolios, at least until 1991 when interest rates began to fall — and bond prices rose.

There is a danger that the swing away from equities has been overdone. For a start, many of the alternative investments which investors have sought since 1987 are essentially short-term. Only shares and real estate can be regarded as long-term investments. This is because equity investments such as shares and real estate give the investor part-ownership of assets. In the case of shares, shareholders own a percentage of the capital of the company; in the case of real estate the interest is often more direct and in one specific property.

Fixed interest investments, however, offer no equity; the investor is merely a lender. Investors are entitled to get back their original capital sum, plus interest which is paid on the loan, but they do not participate in any growth of the organisation. In other words, shares or property can rise in price but fixed interest investments, when redeemed, return only the original amount invested. When inflation has been depreciating the Australian currency by about half every ten years, capital growth becomes an important part of any investment strategy.

FIXED INTEREST INVESTMENTS

Certainly, there are risks in investing in shares or property. But the central argument in this book is that investment risks exist only in the short term. The longer people hold investments such as shares the more certain they are of making money and obtaining real returns from their investment.

INVESTMENT RISKS ARE MAINLY SHORT-TERM

That may seen a platitude or one of the glib sayings spread by stockbrokers to tempt new customers into the market, but it is one of the fundamental truths of the investment business which has been determined, checked and used by the people who frame the investment odds — the actuaries.

Actuaries advise life offices and superannuation funds on probable outcomes over the long term and assess likely long-term assets and liabilities. It is their job to know the odds because they are, in effect, the bookmakers who frame the odds in the investment world.

EVIDENCE OF LONG-TERM RETURNS

This is the result of detailed studies by actuaries produced by the NSW division of the Association of Superannuation Funds of Australia of investment returns:
- In 12 out of 13 five-year periods, the return from shares was above ten per cent. No five-year period showed a negative return and the lowest was 3.9 per cent a year. In all but one of the nine 20-year periods covered, the annual return was more than ten per cent — and at ten

per cent compound a year for 20 years, an original investment increases from $100 to about $800!

- In 11 out of 14 five-year periods, the return from shares was above the rise in the Consumer Price Index, providing 'real' returns. If you lengthen the period to 20 years, shares provided a 'real' return in six out of the nine periods covered
- Even using a more stringent test of inflation — rises in average earnings — share returns outstripped this measure of inflation in all but two of the 20- and 25-year periods.

Over the last available 25-year period to June 1990, shares returned 13.0 per cent a year for that quarter of a century — or 5.1 per cent in 'real' terms after adjusting for the average 7.9 per cent rise in the CPI.

In simple terms, investing in shares over the last 25 years would on average, have turned $100 at the starting point in 1965 into $2600 in 1990 dollars or into $440 in the original 1965 dollars.

Similar results were shown in the total investment returns from a typical superannuation fund portfolio consisting of bonds, shares, overseas and property investments.

So, based on average returns from share investments, anyone who holds shares over ten years is, on the evidence of the last 25 years, certain of finishing in front of the game.

There have been only three periods since 1928 when it has taken more than three years to achieve a positive return from a share investment as measured by the all ordinaries index.

The years from 1937 to 1942 were marked by political instability and then World War II (and price controls on share prices in Australia). After five years during which the value of an average share portfolio declined, by the end of 1941– 42, the six years from June 1936 had shown a slight 2.8 per cent annual compound growth rate. However, for an investor who began a portfolio in June 1936, by the end of a ten-year period in June 1946, the portfolio had risen 89 per cent or an average of 6.6 per cent compound over the ten years.

The second period when it took more than three years in the share market to achieve a positive return was in the

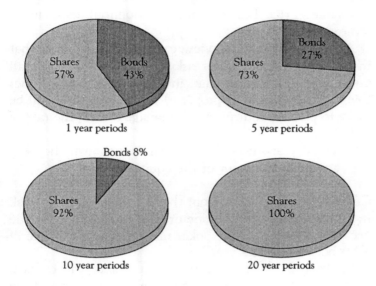

1 year periods   5 year periods

10 year periods   20 year periods

Source: Macquarie Investment Management, from Australian Stock Exchange based on All Ordinaries Accumulation Index and Commonwealth Bank Bond Accumulation Index — 5–10 years.

years from June 1972 to June 1974. An investment made in June 1971 would have depreciated in value to about 71 per cent of its original value by the end of June 1974 before the stock market recovered strongly. But an investor who kept the June 1971 portfolio until June 1979 would have more than doubled the portfolio's value and achieved an average annual compound growth of 10.9 per cent in the eight years to 1979.

These calculations are based on detailed tables of share market returns for years from 1928 to 1993 from the records of the Australian Stock Exchange, as calculated by fund managers Armstrong Jones are available in wall chart forms.

There are other detailed studies over periods of more than 60 years produced by the international actuaries, Frank Russell, which show that over 20-year periods, Australian shares produced a 'real' return of three per cent or more in almost three-quarters of the periods studied. (The 'real' return is after deducting inflation as measured by the Consumer Price Index, from the nominal investment return.)

All this adds up, in my view, to irrefutable evidence that investment in shares is not risky over periods longer than a few years. More than that, investing in anything other than equities (shares or property) in the long term will be lucky to produce returns which manage to beat the rate of inflation.

Over 20 years, doesn't that sound as though the odds are very much in favour of the equity investor?

LOTTO vs EQUITY INVESTMENT

Consider the average person: they might have $5 a week in a Lotto system entry alone or in a pool each week, the occasional flutter on the poker machines and a couple of TAB bets during the year.

For each $1 spent on a Lotto entry, about 40 cents is creamed off by the operators and the government and the odds of winning an average $320,000 first division prize is one chance in 8,145,060. Each $1 bet with a bookmaker sees about 10 to 11 cents disappear into the bookie's bag or into the government's coffers. On the TAB the extent of the rip-off is worse: about 15 to 16 cents is creamed off for the government.

Against that, the 'take' from an equity investment is two or three per cent by stockbrokers or up to six per cent by an investment manager. In the long term, of course, the 'take' by the tax man may also come into the equation for the share investor. Fans of Lotto may note that their winnings are not taxed — neither should they be after the government has taken an initial 40 per cent tax!

People talk about 'investing' in a Lotto entry and each week accept astronomical odds of more than 8 million to one for the big pay-off. This is a nonsense use of the term 'investment'. Lotto players are gambling, in the same way as people who in a boom buy shares they know nothing about.

Yet suggest to regular Lotto gamblers that they invest money in shares and they usually refuse to consider it. It's too risky, they say.

Once again, this is a nonsense which no one seems to understand and certainly no government is willing to explain — as long as people rush lemming-like to spend an estimated $25 billion a year on total gambling in Australia, of which perhaps $2.5 billion is ploughed into lotteries alone.

Against the insecurity of most gambling — and the occasional pay-out from smaller prizes — most investments return some income to the investor, either through interest, dividends, rent or capital gain. People would be far better off investing their $5 or $10 a week which they now gamble on Lotto entries; investment would give them at least some return and the potential advantage of compounding interest. But that would not be as interesting as waiting for the numbers to turn up in an 8 million to one gamble.

Most people seem to gladly accept huge odds in the vain hope of winning the big prize, even though a moment's thought would make them realise that they merely face years of losing their entry money. This Lotto mentality — which accepts absurdly high odds as long as the prize looks big enough — appears to have carried over into everyday attitudes towards saving and investing large sums of money. It is probably part of the reason that lump sum payments are still ingrained in the psyche of most retired people (although, in the past, there was also the effect from taxation rules which encouraged lump sums rather than pensions).

The tendency to chase one in eight million gambles, while avoiding investments which can increase one's wealth over the medium term, is the reason that so few Australians become millionaires via investment.

2

INVESTMENT POSITIVES

Do you sincerely want to be rich? — the bottom line question which the master investment con man of the 1960s, Bernie Cornfeld, used to ask potential IOS (Investor Overseas Services) salesmen.

Small investors and ordinary wage earners can operate in the stock market as well as anyone else, provided they know what they are doing. These days, anyone can become an investor. Virtually every potential type of investment can be accessed by the ordinary person, often directly and nearly always via a managed investment. There is far more information and assistance available and after a decade of inflation averaging more than eight per cent a year there is plenty of incentive.

But the 1987 crash, at least for a few years, reduced the level of investment by individuals. According to a survey by the Australian Stock Exchange (ASX) in 1986, 9.2 per cent of adult Australians (or about 1,013,000 people) owned shares at that time; two years later the number had risen slightly to 1,067,000 but the percentage of adult Australians holding shares had slipped to 9.0 per cent. By the end of 1993 the level had risen from 10.2 per cent in 1991 to an estimated 11.5 to 12 per cent. This followed the two separate public share issues by the Commonwealth Bank of Australia and other large flotations by GIO Australia and Woolworths. These are still relatively low levels compared with the experience in countries such as the UK and the US. There seem to be three main reasons why people don't invest in the share market: a fear of the risks, ignorance of how it works, and lack of money. Contrary to what might be thought, the lack of money is the least important of those reasons, according to successive surveys by the ASX.

Back in the boom time of 1986, the ASX did a national survey which found that the most common reason for not investing in the share market was a lack of understanding of how it worked. About 32 per cent of the answers cited lack of knowledge as the main reason for not investing. Risk came a distant second, with only 25 per cent of people perceiving riskiness. This was perhaps understandable, since the stock market then was nearing the peak of its boom and the crash of 1987 was a year away.

By 1988, October 1987 had shown the riskiness of the stock market and the percentages had almost reversed: almost 39 per cent of people were worried about the risk and only 22 per cent thought their lack of understanding was the main factor.

The most recent results from a late 1991 survey show an interesting trend: there has been a large reduction in the proportion of people worried about risk to just over 28 per cent, but the proportion of people citing lack of knowledge has continued to decline to just above 20 per cent.

It seems that the concerted education programs by the ASX, stockbrokers, financial advisers, investment managers, authors and the media are beginning to take effect, along with the trend towards much higher levels of investment by older and retired people. In addition, the general investing population has, like the rest of the Australian population, become better educated.

With knowledge comes understanding, but it seems that there is still a big gap between understanding how the stock market works and realising the advantages of investing in shares. Risk cannot be eliminated but it can be reduced to minimal levels by using one resource which is available to most people — time.

A stockbroker friend of mine maintains there are only two miracles in the investment world: time and compound interest, and what they achieve together. A typical graph

THE MIRACLE OF COMPOUND INTEREST

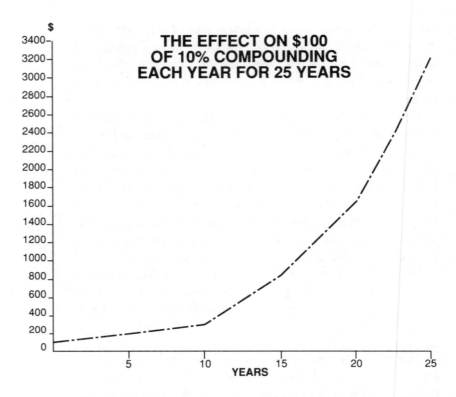

**THE EFFECT ON $100
OF 10% COMPOUNDING
EACH YEAR FOR 25 YEARS**

of an investment which is compounding interest (or dividends) looks something like this:

*ADVANTAGES OF
STARTING EARLY*

There is only one secret to achieving the gains on the compound interest curve at the steeply ascending end; you need to have spent the early years putting in the hard work at the other end. As with many other things in life, you need to start early and work consistently to achieve gains. This is why it is never too early to start investing, either in a fixed interest account or a superannuation fund (where funds can be left to accumulate via compound interest), or in shares where dividends can be reinvested in new shares at a discount to the market price. In fact, the one advantage young people have is time — but they often don't realise this until they have wasted part of their advantage.

Increasingly, more and more people are likely to be given the opportunity to become investors in shares. Many companies now offer employees the opportunity to buy shares, sometimes at a discount to the market price and often on extended terms. Unless there are particular reasons for not investing in the shares, employees should take up these offers.

Several government business organisations (both Federal and State) are planning to follow the Commonwealth Bank's lead in becoming publicly listed companies. This will almost certainly bring new investors to the share market and should prove one of the most fruitful periods for newcomers to the stock market. Too often in the past, newcomers to the stock market have bought at the top of the market and often have bought speculative shares, giving themselves little hope of success.

There also have been new investors brought to the stock exchange via the listing of some former unlisted property trusts. In addition, there have been several large new listed property trusts floated in 1993–94, adding to the variety of listed property investment.

Whenever people start talking about the stock market, the doubters start finding reasons why the average person cannot or should not invest.

MISCONCEPTIONS ABOUT STOCK MARKET INVESTMENT

- 'Shares are only for the rich. You need specialised knowledge. You need to be a big investor.'

This is simply not true, as this book will attempt to convince you. Small investors and ordinary wage and salary earners can operate in the stock market as well as anyone else, provided they think about what they are doing. Of course, they need a little specialised knowledge of market operation (but even the largest and most successful investors needed that at the start). Most people need some expert assistance in the form of a stockbroker or financial adviser to guide them through the maze, but the major requirement is the desire to invest and the innate common sense which most people have. This can be applied just as easily to investing in shares as it can to picking Lotto numbers or choosing a new refrigerator.

- 'You need to be an expert to know when to invest and whether to buy or sell.'

Not so. In the short term and at major turning points the ordinary person's instincts are just as good as picking trends and turning points as the experts. Sometimes they are much better. For instance, there were some gold buffs who were buying gold when prices hit $US800 an ounce early in 1980, but journalists covering the rush into shops at that time reported that there were queues of ordinary people with gold heirlooms and family treasures outside shops. The average person was selling, not buying, because they instinctively recognised that gold was overpriced.

But even if investors do mistime their entry into the stock market the nature of the beast is relatively forgiving, despite what investors might think. A ten-year period usually is enough for the stock market to rise enough to cover up most timing mistakes.

• 'Real estate is the only thing that's worth investing in.'

Not necessarily so. Real estate does have advantages; available figures suggest it provides slightly higher investment returns over the long term than even shares. Surveys of property investments by superannuation funds done by actuaries, Towers Perrin, suggested that commercial property investment had performed well in the long term.

The Towers Perrin surveys found returns of 15.3 per cent a year over the 16 years since the bear market in property in the early 1970s. One alleged advantage of property is supposed to be that it does not fall in price but many people have found out, too late, that this is not true. Of course, it may be true, as salesmen may argue, that if you don't sell when prices fall, as far as the long-term investor is concerned there may well never have been lower prices. But this is a philosophical point only and of little use to an investor who may have to sell in a downturn because of changed circumstances. Property is usually the last asset to fall in price but it also tends to recover in price late in the next upward cycle.

For ordinary investors who are looking at investing in a house or home unit, or a shop or small factory, property has some special attractions: you can see it, walk through it and check on it each week. Real estate, like company shares, represents an investment in real assets which can rise (and fall) in value as well as provide income.

But real estate lacks flexibility. An investment in, say, a home unit, is not as flexible as a parcel of shares. You can't easily sell off part of a home unit to pay your tax bill. Sometimes, it takes months to sell a real estate investment;

at other times, when the market is in the doldrums, real estate can be almost unsaleable except at give-away prices.

Shares are usually more liquid and liquidity is one of the major considerations in any investment. Listed shares are traded every day (if they are a reasonably active issue) and there is a daily price available. This means there is almost immediate liquidity. The drawback to shares is that they can fluctuate in price more sharply than property. This is part of the trade-off necessary to have an investment which can be liquidated quickly.

Investors in unlisted property trusts in 1990 and 1991 discovered that the price which they paid for less volatile values for their security was a lack of liquidity. The combination of units which were often promoted as redeemable at a few weeks notice and assets worth millions which could not be sold without heavy discounts to book values led to freezes on redemptions and to ultimate reforms.

• 'Property is the best long-term investment.'

This is an assertion which many people would support, though many successful share investors would argue otherwise. It is not possible to resolve arguments about the relative merits of shares and property except by resorting to comparisons involving indices and averages — and in most equity investments (particularly real estate) no one buys an index or an average.

Most people have fond memories of the large capital gains they have made on their own house. In many cases, these have been their only capital profits. Many people, however, usually sell only to buy another house, so that the capital gain merely allows them to continue to stay in the housing game at the higher, current prices.

But it is worth considering why most people make money from their own house. The first reason is that they have geared up (or borrowed) to buy the house. A deposit of 25 per cent or less is the usual amount of equity that most home owners put into their purchase and their bank or other lender provides the other 75 per cent of the purchase price. Thus, when property prices increase (thanks to inflation and the passage of time), it is the home owner's equity which benefits from the rise. This is because in most cases the lending institution's loan remains fixed and becomes a declining proportion of the rising value of the property.

The second reason most people make money on their own homes is that they hold their real estate investment for a long time. They buy a house when it is convenient or necessary. They live in it and would rarely consider trading it for another merely to cash in on rising prices or to avoid possible falling prices. They sell only when they need to move or because of a change in their housing needs. Even though many people own several houses in their lifetime, they usually represent a series of stages in one long-term investment.

If investors took the same attitude to quality shares that they take to investment in their own home, they would almost certainly achieve the same sort of long-term capital gains. (In the case of the family home there is one additional advantage: any capital gains are usually not subject to capital gains tax whereas gains on shares or other assets bought after September 1985 are subject to capital gains tax.)

However, there are countless investors who have held leading shares for 25 years or more and who have achieved startling capital gains by doing nothing more than maintaining their holding and banking their dividends twice a year.

- 'There are too many risks in investment. Look at the way people lost money on the stock market after October 1987 and in the Pyramid and Estate Mortgage collapses.'

Certainly, there are risks in investment. The most basic rule (but sometimes the least observed) is that the greater the return, the greater the risk. Safe investment is mostly about recognising this and achieving the best trade-off between risk and return for an individual investor's circumstances.

THE RISKS OF NOT INVESTING

There are also risks in not investing. The greatest risk comes from the effect of inflation, which has averaged about 5 per cent compound over the last ten years, after running at annual rates between 10 and 12 per cent for periods up to the middle 1980s. We have seen a period since the first half of 1991 where inflation has been reduced dramatically to levels of below two per cent. These are levels which we have not seen for more than two decades and are encouraging, but over the long term in Australia those who have assumed that inflation will remain a problem have been correct.

The effect of long-term, persistent inflation is shown in the depreciation of the Australian dollar's purchasing power over the last three decades. Using figures calculated by J.B. Were & Son's research department, from June 1960, $1 shrank in purchasing power to be worth only 78.5 cents by June 1970. In the 1970s, higher inflation cut a swathe through the dollar's purchasing power, so that a 1970 dollar was worth only 37.3 cents in June 1980.

In the 1980s, inflation has abated to below double digits in several years and the improvement is evident in the slower pace of depreciation of the dollar's purchasing power: by June 1993, the 1980 dollar was worth 43 cents.

But no one should get too complacent, because the combined effect of those three decades of inflation has been to reduce the value of $1 in June 1960 to only 12.6 cents in 33 years.

Put the other way, the value of $1 invested in 1960 needed to increase to almost $7.94 by June 1993 merely to maintain its purchasing power in current dollars. That requires an average compound rate of growth of almost 6.5 per cent a year for the 33 years.

INVEST FOR RETIREMENT

Anyone who is 30 years away from retirement should spend a few minutes multiplying all the current prices by eight times to get some idea of the cost of living they could face in retirement if the past level of inflation continues into the next century.

Clearly, with such rates of growth needed to maintain the purchasing power of money, there is a real risk that the value of a person's capital will shrink severely because of inflation, even if it is maintained in nominal terms in a safe bank deposit or fixed interest security. Even interest payments may not keep pace with inflation since it is only in the last few years that interest rates have been 'real' — that is, they have provided a return above the rate of inflation. On top of that, however, taxation on interest earned will reduce the final net, real income.

In the past, people who retired with some retirement benefits did not need to worry unduly if their money ran out; there was always the social security pension to fall back on. That is still the case today, but there already are tests of both incomes and assets designed to concentrate the pension money where it is most needed.

Beyond the short term, however, it is clear that future Federal governments will be unwilling to load future tax-payers with large tax burdens to pay pensions to retired people. After the turn of the century, retired people will represent a growing proportion of the population and a growing burden on government revenue. In other words, only the most needy will be given the safety net of a government pension. Everyone else will have to fend for themselves and the government has spent the last few years emphasising superannuation as the preferred method.

Superannuation has the advantage of some tax concessions and it is a disciplined method. But it is not the only way for people to accumulate the capital necessary for them to live on their own resources during retirement. If people want to maximise their savings during their working life and protect their capital in retirement, they will need to have an investment plan, either through superannuation or by using their own resources.

In short, in the future, people will need to be investors — one way or another — to make sure they are survivors.

3

SHOPPING FOR INVESTMENTS

Eighty per cent of success is showing up.

— Woody Allen

*T*he investment world these days resembles a groaning smorgasbord of investment products and the first reaction of the novice investor is to feel acute indigestion. This is understandable since the national table of listed shares in the *Australian Financial Review* runs to eight pages, including exotic fare like options and futures. The listing of retail managed investment products in the fortnightly investment paper, *Money Management*, runs to seven tabloid news pages.

But, just as a smorgasbord is meant only to provide a selection of food dishes, so the investment smorgasbord is designed mainly to give investors every conceivable variety of investment choices. Any balanced meal will consist of two or more different courses, with choices of dishes in each course. If the investment smorgasbord is rearranged into different courses, it starts to become a little more digestible for most people.

The main distinction in the investment menu is between fixed interest and equity investments. This distinction (which we discussed in the first chapter) is as basic as the distinction in a restaurant menu between meat and fish.

Fixed interest securities — such as bonds, debentures, bank bills and deposits — are essentially loans to a finan-

* Interim dividend higher: cover based on previous year's earning rate.
‡ Interim dividend lower: cover based on previous year's earning rate.
$ Bonus issue since balancing date: cover for dividend based on last year's profit figures.
f Indicates that the current dividend contains some degree of franking.

INDUSTRIAL LEADERS

52 week High	Low	Company par value	MARKET Last Sale	+ or -	Buy	Sell	Div'd ¢ share	Tms cov	Net asset back	Div yld %	P.E. ratio
4.80	3.33	A.G.L.$1	4.00	+7	4.00	4.05	18.00	1.34	2.48	4.50	16.6
2.12	1.55	APronews40c	1.67	+8	1.65	1.65	5.70 f	1.58	.79	3.41	18.6
1.45	.58	AAPC50c	1.06	+4	1.06	1.06	1.10	2.91	1.04	1.04	33.1
3.80	1.46	AConPress50c	3.98	+4	3.96	3.98	28.00	1.25	5.09	7.04	11.4
2.55	1.46	ANI30c	1.80		1.78	1.80	9.00 f	1.02	.62	5.00	19.6
5.72	3.67	ANZ$1	3.90	+6	3.88	3.90	21.00	.64	3.43	5.38	28.9
2.40	1.39	AdelBton50c	1.49	+2	1.50	1.55	9.00 f	1.13	1.99	6.04	14.6
1.496	1.246	AdvPP1.37	1.34		1.34	1.36	11.60	1.00	1.37	8.66	11.6
11.94	7.95	Advance Bk$1	8.90	+10	8.88	8.90	60.00	1.10	5.07	6.74	13.5
2.50	1.35	Alcan$1	1.34		2.45	2.45			2.11		5.8
11.12	8.05	Amcor$1	8.88	+13	8.86	8.92	32.00 f	1.83	2.58	3.60	15.2
2.98	2.35	Argo$1	2.67	+7	2.67	2.69	12.50 f	1.00	2.87	4.68	21.3
12.62	7.85	Arnotts50c	7.90		7.82	7.90	29.00	.99	1.81	3.67	27.4
.553	.40	Aust Con25c	.49	+1	.48	.49			.07		8.2
2.54	1.95	A Found50c	2.13	+10	2.12	2.12	10.00	.80	2.18	4.69	26.8
13.98	10.60	BHP$1	18.22	+6	18.22	18.22	44.00 f	2.11	6.43	8.15	19.6
1.89	1.50	BTProp T1.50	1.62	-4	1.62	1.66	13.20	1.00	1.72		12.3
3.58	2.15	BTR Nylex50c	2.82		2.82	2.85	11.00	1.37	1.29	5.90	18.7
5.65	4.50	Bank Qld$1	4.50	-19	4.57	4.80	23.00 f	1.37	2.54	5.11	14.3
7.20	4.40	Bank Melb$1	4.60	+10	4.60	4.80	28.00	1.80	3.48	6.09	9.1
4.561	2.863	Boral50c	3.30	+3	3.30	3.30	20.00 f	1.21	2.08	6.06	13.6
15.60	11.80	Brambles$1	13.12	-2	13.06	13.12	60.00		5.39	4.57	
40.52	26.00	Brickwork20c	27.00		26.00	26.80	100.00 f	1.46	21.20	3.70	18.5
1.18	.83	Brierley41c	1.00	+4	1.09	1.01	7.38	1.20	.94		11.3
10.62	6.65	Bunnings$1	10.40	+10	10.40		34.00 f	1.17	3.83	3.27	26.1
5.03	3.45	Burns P50c	3.46	-2	3.47	3.49	18.00	1.54	2.62	5.20	12.5
1.95	1.23	Burswood50c	1.55	-2	1.52	1.55	17.00	1.00	1.36	10.97	9.1
11.24	5.12	CCAmatil50c	8.20	+16	8.22	8.30	18.00 f	1.42	2.87	2.20	32.1
5.456	3.82	CSR$1	4.82	+6	4.82	4.82	25.00 f	1.34	3.31	5.19	14.3
3.50	2.20	Caltex$1	3.33	+13	3.15	3.33	10.00 f	3.00	4.16	1.11	
2.691	2.271	Capital P$1	2.60		2.60	2.62	18.10	2.44		6.96	14.4
3.35	2.32	CartHolt41c	2.30	+8	3.05	3.10	6.56	2.41	1.88	2.11	19.3
3.85	2.35	Chal Bank$1	3.30	+10	3.20	3.30	20.00 f	1.13	2.11	6.06	14.7
2.75	1.34	Clyde50c	2.00		2.20	2.25	8.50	.94	1.15	3.78	28.1
5.70	4.04	ColesMyer50c	4.13	-8	4.15	4.15	19.50 f	1.56	2.49	4.72	23.6
5.75	3.45	Comalco$1	5.25	+14	5.25	5.25	6.00	2.35	2.00	4.50	37.2
10.20	7.35	CwthBank$2	7.76	+14	7.73	7.76	46.00	1.12	5.93		52.2
3.70	1.539	E.R.G.Aus20c	3.34	-1	3.34	3.35					53.2
6.02	3.473	Email50c	4.54		4.52	4.54	24.00 f	1.42	1.89	5.35	13.3
1.40	.60	FAI10c			2.47	2.47	7.00	1.36	.83	3.28	
3.45	2.20	Farfax50c	2.47	+10	2.45	2.47	7.00	1.85	2.08	2.39	25.9
9.40	5.50	Faulding50c	6.70		6.65	6.95	16.00 f	1.77	2.45	3.64	22.6
3.21	1.696	Fletcher ordiv32c	2.91	-1	2.91	2.95	10.60		3.67	5.19	15.5
9.21	4.18	Foodland50c	5.26		5.20	5.20	20.00		3.55		
1.60	1.86	Foster $1	1.01	+1	1.01	1.02	18.10	1.78		5.34	9.4
3.07	1.103	Foster $1	2.45	+1	2.44	2.45	10.00	1.00	3.41	5.31	18.8
1.55	2.27	Franki20c	1.26	+1	1.26	1.27	3.00	2.63	.58	5.60	15.9
3.60	2.33	GIO Aust$1	2.34	+5	2.33	2.34	19.60	1.26	6.84		11.6
2.95	1.69	GPT$1	2.47		2.45	2.47	16.00	1.00	2.72	7.84	12.6
2.06	1.24	GemRetail$2	1.74	+1	1.72	1.74	14.84	1.00	1.87	8.53	11.7
1.78	2.04	Goodman50c	1.26	+1	1.26	1.27	12.00 f	.95	1.30	8.73	12.1
2.85	3.312	Hardie J$1	2.10	+3	2.08	2.10	12.00 f	.32	.96	5.71	53.8
4.85		Harvey20c	4.10	+10	4.00	4.10	6.95	2.82		1.70	21.0

52 week High	Low	Company par value	MARKET Last Sale	+ or -	Buy	Sell	Div'd ¢ share	Tms cov	Net asset back	Div yld %	P.E. ratio
1.50	1.30	Heath Ins25c	1.32	+2	1.32	1.38	10.00 f	2.28	1.09	7.58	5.8
11.50	7.15	ICI$1	10.70	+20	10.70	10.98	27.00 f		3.91	2.52	26.9
5.90	4.26	Incitec$1	5.50	+15	5.50	5.50	26.00 f	1.18	1.86	4.73	17.9
2.92	2.64	Jupiters25c	2.92	+5	2.90	2.90	17.50 f	1.20	1.99	5.99	13.9
2.60	1.74	Leighton50c	1.99	+3	1.99	2.30	8.00	.95	1.28	4.02	26.2
19.20	14.92	L.Lease50c	16.12	+4	16.04	16.12	77.00	1.34	9.21	4.78	15.7
3.40	2.40	Lionnathan20c	2.60	+5	2.60	2.64	11.60	1.92	2.45	4.46	11.7
10.04	7.11	Mayne N50c	7.78	+12	7.76	7.78	31.00	1.17	2.57	3.98	21.4
4.21	3.17	Metal Man50c	3.18	-2	3.14	3.18	14.00 f	1.61	1.56	4.40	14.1
4.28	3.17	MtwayBank50c	3.87	+7	3.87	3.95	21.00	1.22	1.86	5.43	15.1
6.78	4.28	Mildara50c	6.05	+15	5.95	5.95	23.00 f	1.37	1.99	3.80	19.2
13.14	9.63	Nat Aust$1	10.68	+10	10.66	10.68	61.00 f	1.43	5.77	5.71	15.2
2.05	1.48	Nat Foods50c	1.92	+2	1.91	1.92	7.25 f	1.59	.80	3.78	16.7
.91		NatMutP1$1	.87		.86	.87	6.48		6.07	7.45	16.7
12.00	7.45	News Corp50c	8.44	+16	8.40	8.44	14.00 f	19.00	2.26	.36	13.4
6.28	3.31	Nine Net$1	4.28	-7	4.28	4.30	11.50 f	1.69	.62	3.27	14.8
2.70	2.05	OPSM Pr50c	2.20	+7	2.18	2.20		1.15		5.23	16.7
1.35	1.35	Orbital50c	1.48	+12	1.48	1.48		.46			
4.62	2.82	P Meg Prmt50c	2.82	+4	2.82	2.85	20.40 f	1.25	2.15	7.23	11.0
2.63	4.13	Pac BBA$1	3.60	+12	3.56	3.60	10.50 f	1.64	1.64	2.92	20.9
5.92	1.06	Pac Dunlp50c	4.19	+4	4.18	4.19	21.00 f	1.22	1.16	5.01	16.3
1.38	4.55	Palm Tube50c	1.13	+10	1.10	1.13	6.00 f	1.15	.86	5.31	24.0
5.76	2.19	Perp Tst$1	5.10	+10	5.01	5.10	29.00 f	1.15	3.45	5.69	15.3
3.42		Pion.Int50c	2.88	+4	2.85	2.88	15.00 f	1.05	1.78	5.21	18.3
6.96	4.50	QBE$1	4.72	-8	4.71	4.76	16.00 f	2.42	2.77	3.39	12.2
3.94	2.85	QUF50c	2.90	+15	2.89	2.90	14.50 f	1.51	1.64	5.00	14.1
7.70	5.20	Rothmans$1	5.40		5.30	5.35	40.00 f	1.47	3.47	3.41	8.9
5.60	3.40	Rur.Press$1	4.85	+5	4.75	4.85	15.00 f	1.23	2.17	3.09	14.3
2.80	2.20	Schro PF$1	2.32	+18	2.28	2.32				8.62	9.5
4.40	2.60	Seven Net50c	3.20	+10	3.20	3.24	8.00	.91	1.64	4.61	23.8
8.00	3.12	Simsmetal50c	6.08	+18	6.04	6.08	28.00 f	1.16	2.35	4.44	13.4
36.61	5.15	Smith Hwd$1	6.20	+10	6.14	6.20	45.00 f	3.39	12.59	1.80	16.7
7.101	25.00	Soul Pat$1	25.00		25.00	26.00					19.7
3.96	2.70	Southcorp50c	2.74	-1	2.74	2.75	16.25 f	1.22	.81	5.93	10.1
1.80	1.15	Spotless50c	1.20	+2	2.74	1.45	8.50 f	1.12	.68	7.92	10.3
1.63	1.425	Spot Serv25c	1.50	+3	1.62	1.62		1.00		6.30	15.2
5.498	5.425	St.George$1	5.62	+5	5.62	5.62	42.00 f		4.32	7.47	11.9
3.70	3.00	Stockland1.10	3.21	+5	3.04	3.07	24.00 f	1.00	2.25	7.82	12.7
2.52	1.80	TNT50c	2.61	+11	2.20	2.21			.61		
4.23	2.85	Tubemaker50c	3.95		3.98	2.98	7.00 f	1.32	1.65	3.32	22.7
1.12	3.05	Tyco20c	2.95	-7	2.89	2.95	7.00	3.14	1.11	7.37	4.3
3.48	5.70	Village R50c	3.48	-7	3.48	3.58	18.00 f	2.23	.64	5.17	29.7
4.30		WA News50c	4.15	+10	4.13	4.15	33.00	1.03	2.50	7.95	12.2
4.75		Wattyl50c	5.80	+5	5.78	5.80	20.00 f	1.88	2.54	3.45	15.4
7.85	9.32	Wesfarmers50c	8.40	+10	8.36	8.40	32.00 f	1.23	2.54	3.81	21.4
9.32	6.80	Wfield H$1	7.40		7.50	7.50	12.75 f	2.95	4.64	1.72	19.7
6.80	2.27	Wfield Tr.	2.36	+3	2.34	2.36	18.79	1.00	2.32	7.96	12.6
2.95	5.20	Weston G50c	7.90		7.90	8.00	16.50 f	3.35	4.62	2.09	14.3
9.20	3.67	Westpac$1	4.34	+14	4.31	4.34	14.00	1.42	3.56	3.23	434.0
3.52	2.602	Woolwrths25c	2.85	+7	2.84	2.85	12.00 f		.59	4.21	16.7
1.90	1.46	Wpac Prop	1.83	+1	1.82	1.83	16.00	1.42	1.68	8.74	–

cial institution. The lender or investor receives an agreed rate of interest (which is often fixed) and at the end of the term of the investment is entitled only to the return of their original capital (plus interest if this has been not paid out or compounded).

Equities — such as shares, real estate and managed investment products invested in these areas — give an investor a stake in the assets. The returns, either in dividends or rent, are not guaranteed and, like the market value of the assets, can rise or fall depending on economic and investment conditions.

The profusion of managed investment products offered to the public reflects the same sort of approach which produces the thousands of items stocked at the average supermarket.

This analogy was chosen not only because it was apt but because of what one of the fathers of investment, Benjamin Graham, said more than 30 years ago: 'You buy shares like you buy groceries, not the way you buy perfume. You're looking for value.'

Of course, in the real-world grocery supermarket, manufacturers and retailers do not know precisely what each individual shopper wants, so they produce a range of most types of products, in the most popular colours and flavours. The same thing happens in the area of managed equity investment products where there is a bewildering variety of different products.

Investors, therefore, should regard their task in shopping for investments in the same way as they approach their regular trip to the supermarket. They are free to wheel their trolleys through the store, taking whatever products they fancy. But they will have to pay at the final checkout for their own choices. Above all, they will do much better in the investment supermarket if they have sat down beforehand and made out a sensible shopping list.

DECIDE ON YOUR INVESTMENT AIM

This means investors should understand a little about the products on offer as well as realising just what they are trying to achieve from their investment program. To keep this book within reasonable confines, I've assumed that investors have been through the initial check list and, perhaps after reading the first two chapters, have decided that they do need a long-term investment program. In summary, this plan may range from assuring their capital and keeping it on hand for ready use, through to investment leading to long-term growth in savings to provide for a comfortable retirement.

However small their initial investment, investors have to decide what they want from their investment. It is pointless investing funds in the stock market which really are earmarked for some purpose in 6 or 12 months, or to leave long-term savings in an at-call bank deposit.

COMPARISON OF FIXED INTEREST SECURITIES AND EQUITIES

It also is important, in the process of selecting investment products from the menu, to avoid the trap of thinking in investment stereotypes. It is easy to characterise fixed interest investments as stodgy, conservative and uninteresting, and to think of ordinary shares as dynamic, highly profitable and even sexy. There is a danger that we could see the fixed interest securities as the tortoise and shares as the hare. The hare certainly was in front for several decades but in the ten years to the end of 1990 returns from bonds actually beat returns from shares.

This was only a brief change in the long-term trend. Figures for 1991 showed shares had edged back in front of bonds. However, even after the boom 1993 period on the share market, the outperformance of shares in the 10 years to the end of 1993 was less than 1 per cent as the following table shows:

INVESTMENT RETURNS — SHARES VERSUS BONDS

Return (% p.a.) for year to December 1993	1 year	5 years	10 years
Ordinary shares	45.4	13.0	15.7
Government bonds	16.5	16.6	15.0

Sources: Sedwick Noble Lowndes; share returns based on ASX All Ordinaries Accumulation index; bond returns based on Commonwealth Bank bond index.

COMPARATIVE RETURNS — THE LAST FOUR YEARS

Year	Shares	Bonds
1990	−17.5%	+18.3%
1991	+34.2%	+24.4%
1992	−2.3%	+10.2%
1993	+45.4%	+16.5%
Four year average	+12.0%	+17.3%

Clearly, bonds managed to keep pace with inflation which averaged 7 per cent a year in the decade to 1991, falling to 5.3 per cent a year in the 10 years to 1993. In the 10 years to the end of 1993, bonds would have produced a total return of $405 for each $100 originally invested. In the same period, the return of 15.7 per cent for shares would have produced about a final figure of $430 for each $100 invested in shares. To maintain the purchasing power of $100 in line with 5.3 per cent a year inflation, the capital needed to rise to $168 in the 10 years.

In case anyone has begun to fall in love with bonds, it is worth remembering the very long-term results in investment. Based on figures from the same source, it can be shown that over a 60-year period to 1989, shares have produced almost twice as much as bonds — actually, 10.5 per cent a year compared with 5.6 per cent a year from 1928 to 1989.

Similarly, long-term measures of investment returns from the turn of this century by actuaries, Frank Russell, show that there has been no 20-year period in which bonds have outperformed shares.

This general picture of outperformance is also shown by the long-term figures from the NSW division of the Association of Superannuation Funds of Australia (ASFA). In the 25 years to the end of June 1989, bonds produced an average annual return of only 7.8 per cent, compared with shares which produced an annual return of 13.9 per cent.

The comparison between shares and fixed interest debentures shows a similar outperformance. Stockbrokers J.B. Were & Son have been comparing investment in shares with company debentures for many years. Over the 20 years to 30 April 1993 the results are clearly in favour of shares which produced total returns 3.6 times as large as those from debentures.

In the past five years, the growth in the returns from shares has slowed but shares still beat debentures by a factor of 1.8 to 1 in the latest ten-year period.

The Were study is a fairly realistic one for ordinary investors to consider, since it does not compare a theoretical parcel of a hundred or more shares in the all ordinaries index with bonds. Instead, it compares returns from ten-year debentures (initially Citicorp Australia and more recently, Australian Guarantee Corporation) with returns from ten shares which many ordinary investors are likely to hold. In addition, the study does not assume reinvestment of the dividends or interest payments. While many shareholders now routinely reinvest dividends through dividend reinvestment plans, this has not been the usual pattern for most of the past 20 years. The Were study therefore understates the effect of growth in capital and dividends by simply adding the income stream and the capital gain and not compounding the gains.

As we will see, there is a price to be paid for higher returns. This is the higher level of risk inherent in some forms of investment. For most people just coming to investment, risk means the chance of losing all or part of their capital. This is more usually the fate of money which is being gambled, rather than invested.

Rather, investment experts measure risk largely by the volatility in returns (technically, the standard deviation from the average return). For the present, it is enough to note that both bonds and shares (or fixed interest and equities) have their place in investment portfolios.

MAKING A CHOICE

The major task often is to decide just when to chase the hare-like returns from shares and when to be content with the steady, tortoise-like attributes of bonds.

This is a lot harder in practice than it seems. It is easy to look back on the last ten years but it is a lot harder to look into the future and predict investment conditions accurately, particularly when conditions in the financial system have been subject to much more rapid rates of change. After the unusually long outperformance by bonds in the last few years, many now think shares will resume as the pace-maker — but at lower rates of return.

In the early 1990s there was a growing theory that the world and Australia were moving into a period of lower inflation and that this might help bond returns to improve in coming years. If, for example, there is very low or limited inflation, then some people might prefer to reduce their reliance on shares and swap the volatility in returns from shares for the stability of fixed interest capital values.

There are other theories which suggest that 'real' returns from bonds and fixed interest investments (that is, the return after deducting inflation) may remain high for some time. In general, there is a potential capital shortage in the world with huge demand likely for capital from Eastern Europe and the former Soviet Union and other rapidly developing economies. In Australia, there is a feeling that our 'real' interest rates may have to remain high to continue to attract overseas capital to underwrite our capital deficit with the rest of the world.

However, the key for anyone contemplating long-term investment is the long-term outlook for inflation beyond, say, the next two or three years. While all investors would welcome permanent low inflation, the long-term trends suggest that backing bonds over shares in the long term would be going against the odds.

In only three of the 13 five-year periods studied by the ASFA actuaries did bonds beat share returns. In all three cases it was by relatively narrow margins — 1.3 per cent versus 0.9 per cent in the five years to June 1977, 6.2 per cent versus 3.8 per cent in the five years to June 1978 and by 14.0 per cent versus 12.2 per cent in the five years to June 1985. In all the other five-year periods, shares outperformed bonds by sometimes massive amounts. In the ten-year periods, bonds beat shares in only one of the 13 periods and matched shares in one other decade. If the period is extended to 15, 20 or 25 years, in no recent period did bonds outperform shares.

The performance figures also provide another lesson: results will depend very much on the start and end points chosen. Take those figures for the ten years to the end of 1990, for example. The starting point in December 1980, for instance, was within a month of the peak of a six-year rise in the market from September 1974. The all ordinaries index had more than 40 per cent to fall before it reached its July 1982 low point in the middle of the 1982–83 recession. Then, it rose more than five-fold in the largest bull market yet seen in Australia, before losing ground from its peak levels in the 1987–90 downturn.

This was the sequence of yearly returns from the AMP equity fund for superannuation investors as reported by actuaries Noble Lowndes:

1981	–8.8%
1982	–8.5%
1983	+55.7%
1984	–7.4%
1985	+45.6%
1986	+44.5%
1987	–2.3%
1988	+18.3%
1989	+21.1%
1990	–12.6%
1991	+32.5%
1992	–3.6%
1993	+41.8%

These returns would have been a typical picture of the performance of an average investor's share portfolio over the 13 year period. Little wonder that, by the start of 1987, investors were hypnotised by shares because, in the five years to 1986, every $100 invested in the AMP equity fund had increased to more than $320. These results were by no means abnormal among other managers.

In the period since 1986, share investors have experienced three 'down' years, offset by four years of growth of 18 per cent a year or more. As a result — and despite a total of six 'down' years out of 13 years — $100 invested at the start of the period would now be worth $564. That represents an annual compound rate of return which averages just over 14 per cent a year over the 13 year period.

The experts have developed a model of cycles in the economy which often depicts the various stages on a clock face. (A graphic representation of a trade cycle 'clock' is shown below, and was compiled by the London Evening Standard from a study of trade cycles over 150 years. It is reproduced from a Jardine Fleming publication.) This model, in various guises, was being used early in 1991 by a wide range of people to encourage investors back into the market. It shows that the first sign that a boom has reached its top is when interest rates begin to rise. That would normally start to see bond prices ease in value, closely followed by a decline in share prices. It is only later in the cycle that real estate prices begin to fall. Falling interest rates then become the trigger for a recovery in investments with bonds and then shares rising in price and, according to this model, real estate prices taking the longest to recover. The key to profiting from these cycles is the length of time occupied by falling or rising asset prices and interest rates.

The theory of switching from the best-performing asset just as it peaks into the investment which is taking over the running is fine in theory. In practice, some investors and managers will get part of the timing right but, as October 1987 showed, they only have to mistime moving out of a major share boom by one day to blow away much of their past success.

As a result, most professional managers these days rely on having a balanced portfolio, to which they make constant fine adjustments, readjusting the distribution of assets within the portfolio, buying when they look cheap and selling some when they look overpriced. Generally, these balanced investors will have a mixture of cash, bonds, shares, property and overseas investments. They aim to produce a final, acceptable return based on the argument that what you might lose on the swings you make up on the roundabouts.

A BALANCED PORTFOLIO

There is nothing wrong with attempting to pick turning points in major markets and some of the better-performing investment managers have been these so-called 'market timers'. Bankers Trust Australia (BTA) is perhaps the classic example; in 1987 its managers decided that share markets as a whole were dangerously overpriced and they hedged their exposure to the world's share markets through the futures and options markets. Effectively, when the crash came, they were holding much lower percentages of shares than most other managers. This instance of cor-

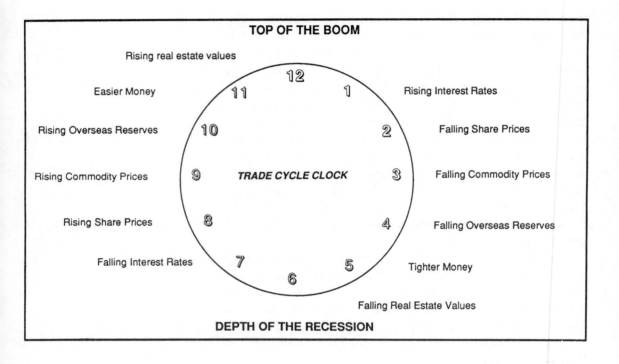

TOP OF THE BOOM

Rising real estate values

Easier Money

Rising Overseas Reserves

Rising Commodity Prices

Rising Share Prices

Falling Interest Rates

TRADE CYCLE CLOCK

Rising Interest Rates

Falling Share Prices

Falling Commodity Prices

Falling Overseas Reserves

Tighter Money

Falling Real Estate Values

DEPTH OF THE RECESSION

rectly picking the market played a major part in putting BTA well ahead of its competing managers for several years after the October 1987 crash. Even the managers at BTA, though, would not claim to be able to pick the exact turning points of investment markets on a regular basis (though many investors now use BTA as a manager who tends to add value to portfolios by using this market timing approach).

In a sense, most investors will probably win (as Woody Allen suggests) simply by turning up for the game: they will finish up doing better than the person who does not save at all or the saver who does not invest their savings wisely. About the only time when savers with cash on short-term deposit manage to outperform investors is during a severe recession or depression when all asset prices except cash are falling.

PLAYING THE INVESTMENT GAME

There is a difference between the way the professional and amateur investors play the game. According to an American investment management expert, Dr Charles D. Ellis, investment is like playing tennis; tennis champions beat their opponents by producing winning strokes consistently — a winner's game. But amateur tennis players win social matches because they make fewer errors than their opponents — a loser's game.

Most performances in the investment game are judged against benchmarks of the general performance of the market as a whole. For example, an investment manager who runs a portfolio of shares will be judged against the all ordinaries accumulation index as produced by the Australian Stock Exchange (ASX). This index measures the capital growth of share prices across the whole share list and it assumes that, as in many managed investments like super-annuation, dividends are reinvested back into more shares.

There are now so many professional investment managers who are proficient at their business that the winners among the professional managers are those who make the fewest mistakes. In other words, those who take the approach of a social tennis player in trying to keep the ball in play may do better than those who try, like the tennis pros, to hit winners close to the sidelines.

The point for the ordinary investor in what Dr Ellis is saying is that they now have an easy choice in long-term investments. They can place their funds with professional investment managers and let them play the professional game, generally producing average returns. Alternatively, they can do much of the investment themselves and play the sort of investment game which suits their needs and their personality.

It is, perhaps, unusual to think of investment as a game. In recent years, investment has been a very serious business of making money (serious both for the investors and for those who manage the investments). It has also been the means of losing money for many people. Only the most cynical players thought it was a game, and yet John Maynard Keynes, the man whose economic theories still influence many people, talked about investment as a game in his *General Theory of Employment, Interest and Money* back in 1936. He said, 'The game of professional investment is intolerably boring and over-exacting to anyone who is entirely exempt from the gambling instinct.' That distaste for the gamblers in the investment world did not prevent

Keynes from playing the markets shrewdly enough to replenish the coffers of King's College, Cambridge.

Investment may be a more serious game than a social game of tennis or golf for some people, but there is no need for the amateur investor to be too intimidated. Certainly, investment can be approached seriously and reverently, and it can be treated as a science, but it can also be treated as an art and practised even by those without formal training. It even can be played as a game and, at the very least, it can become an absorbing hobby for many people.

4

THE BUSINESS OF INVESTMENT MANAGEMENT

The first rule of investment is: don't lose. And the second rule is: don't forget the first rule. And that's all the rules there are.

— *Warren Buffett, US investment manager and recent chairman of Salomon Brothers*

*A*nyone who is considering investing in the share market needs to know something about the investment styles and processes used by professional investment managers. This will not necessarily produce instant riches for a new investor but it will help them to understand how investment managers can shape the trends, fashions and even patterns in the share market.

Books and busts usually do more than make or lose money for people; they also cause major re-assessments of investment thinking. Each time the share market falls in a heap after a burst of enthusiasm, people who have hired investment managers to get the best returns on their money start asking awkward questions. This certainly happened in late 1987 when many superannuation funds found themselves facing large, immediate losses in their investment portfolios.

But it had happened in 1974 as well, when superannuation funds had just begun to have their investments managed by life offices using relatively rudimentary methods which are generally referred to as the EFG approach. 'EFG' refers to the system pioneered by the National Mutual group, covering Equity, Fixed interest and Growth units, which superannuation funds could buy from the various

LESSONS FROM CRASHES

life offices. The superannuation fund trustees, in effect, had to decide their own mix of asset classes for their portfolio. These portfolios are usually called 'balanced portfolios' and include a diversified range of investments in an attempt to balance the needs of investors to achieve income, growth and a lack of volatility.

But investors discovered that if they were holding the wrong balance of investments at the time of a crash, they lost money. A fortunate few discovered that their managers had taken an active management approach and they did not lose as much as other people. In both 1974 and 1987, superannuation trustees discovered terms like 'asset allocation' and 'active management' — though in 1987 there was now a much wider recognition of the process.

ACTIVE vs PASSIVE MANAGEMENT

In 1974, the investment managers were asking the superannuation funds to make all the decisions on the right mixture of assets. In 1987, we had almost the opposite; the investment managers had taken over most of the process of choosing the mix of assets within the funds they were offering. By then, most investment managers in Australia were active managers, meaning that they adjusted the mix of assets in the total portfolio as they thought appropriate, reducing the proportion in shares if they thought the share market was too high, for example, or increasing overseas investments if they feared a depreciation of the Australian currency.

That sort of approach is perhaps the sort of approach most people would instinctively take. And you might think it should have ensured that many funds didn't get caught in the October 1987 crash. But by 1987, the combination of a boom and the chase for the best returns by trustees of superannuation funds contributed to what essentially became a case of the greedy leading the greedy. Few people were concerned with the risks when returns were so high, as shown by exposures of 50 to 60 per cent of some pooled funds to the booming share market.

When the crash came in October 1987, what superannuation fund trustees and other investors wanted to know was how they could avoid getting caught like that again. All the investment managers, of course, were frantically applying their resources to answering that question as

quickly and as convincingly as possible. Those who produced the right answers have survived; those who did not
and could not explain convincingly what they were doing
lost funds and clients.

Since then, there has been an explosion of debate and
research on how to master the risks of investment. As a
result, the Australian investment management business
has become very sophisticated, very quickly. But this does
not necessarily mean that we have reached the ultimate
in investment knowledge; in investment, as in so many
other human pursuits, the more you learn, the more you
realise there is to learn.

What has emerged, however, is a whole new language.
We now see investment managers classified as 'active' or
'passive'; there is a debate about the relative merits of
quantitative and qualitative analysis (analysis based only
on numbers or analysis using judgments as well as data);
styles of investment managers are now analysed and investors can choose between managers taking a 'top-down' or a
'bottom-up' approach.

Most Australian investment managers are still 'active'
managers; they adjust the combination of assets and
attempt to pick the best-performing shares. Every quarter,
say, the managers will look at the economic factors ahead
and may re-adjust the mix of assets.

At the other extreme, there are some managers who have
adopted a 'passive' approach, the opposite of active management. The manager decides an asset allocation which
best appears to balance the risk and returns (based on long-
term history) and apportions the funds, usually reweighting
the portfolio regularly. In some purely passive funds linked
to, say, a share index like the all ordinaries index, the
manager buys (and adjusts) the mix of individual shares to
produce a result as close as possible to the performance of
the market index.

PASSIVE MANAGEMENT

This seems, at first sight, a defeatist approach and many
active managers still condemn such an extreme approach.
They claim the passive approach (based as it is on past
performances) depends for its success on history repeating
itself. It certainly involves the trustees of the fund, helped
by their investment consultants, in making the decisions

on where to invest assets, a decision which in an active portfolio is taken by the investment manager.

Against that criticism, those favouring passive asset allocation and less active management argue that over the long-term it is unlikely that even half of the active managers will beat the market average returns.

(According to figures supplied by funds management research group, ASSIRT, for actively managed share growth trusts, only 25 out of 62 or about 40 per cent of the managers outperformed the all ordinaries accumulation index in the three years to 1993, excluding gold and resources trusts).

In the short term, it is picking winners of stocks which will enable an investor to outperform the market average. But this gets into the field of speculation which raises the risk factor in a portfolio substantially. In the long term, however, most active managers who indulge in only limited speculative purchases or timing switches have difficulty in outperforming the index.

There is also an argument that managers may do better if they have a 'core' in their portfolio which is weighted to track the market index. Around this, they add other elements of a balanced portfolio, designed to benefit from the expected economic and market conditions.

In fact, few professional investment managers these days are purely active or purely passive. This is partly to do with the approach needed to market themselves, but it is mainly to do with the desire of most managers and their clients to find the best mix of all investment techniques. BT Australia, which is one of the most aggressive, active, bottom-up managers, also does a lot of work on quantitative analysis to tailor portfolios to clients' tolerance to volatility in results.

Not even the most aggressive active managers will be confident enough in their own forecasting to make a 100 per cent bet on picking the right movement in the market by, say, switching entirely from shares to short-term cash holdings. But many might readjust their portfolio by altering the percentage held in an asset class within a range which has been agreed by the superannuation fund's trustees. There also are few purely passive managers. Things can change — for instance, dividend imputation can make shares look better value or a fall in inflation can make bonds look a better investment.

But there is much more to investment management theory than the active versus passive debate. Perhaps the next most fundamental differences are those between 'stock selection' and 'asset allocation'. These approaches, in turn, typify managers using either a 'bottom-up' or a 'top-down' style of managing investments.

The top-down or asset allocation approach generally involves deciding on a range of percentage holdings in assets such as fixed interest securities, Australian shares, direct property holdings, overseas shares and short-term cash. These percentages are framed, after the trustees of funds decide on the level of risk they are prepared to accept. Then, with the broad asset allocations decided, individual shares, properties or bonds are then selected. Thus the portfolio is decided from the 'top down', depending on a view of the economy and markets.

THE TOP-DOWN APPROACH

Research generally has show that most investment gains come from asset allocation rather than stock selection; the general view is that 70 to 90 per cent of gains come from asset allocation and the minority of gains come from selecting stocks (though this has been less true in the last few years). Thus, some investment managers will limit the shares in their portfolios to those regarded as the best-performing, the best value, the safest, and the most marketable. Alternatively, many investment managers weight their portfolios generally in line with one of several market indices.

This is a recognition that most clients like to see performance at least as good as the all ordinaries index. The approach usually is to buy stocks so that they represent about the same weighting in the portfolio as they do in the all-ordinaries index. But managers then finetune their portfolios by holding more or less of individual stocks they think will outperform or underperform the market as a whole.

So, if a particular bank comprises 1 per cent of the index and the manager prefers it to another bank, he might overweight by increasing the percentage holding to 1.5 per cent of the portfolio and reducing the weighting of another bank. Many stockbrokers and other researchers, in turn, frame their recommendations with this in mind, suggesting 'market weight', 'over-weighting' or 'under-weighting' for individual stocks.

This means that many investment managers in Australia have a share portfolio which closely tracks the all ordinaries index or, even more to the point, the 50 Leaders index. Inevitably, because they are making very few large bets on picking stocks, the performance of most managers tends towards the average over a longer period of time which, once again, helps produce the situation where few managers, active or otherwise, consistently outperform the market average.

This, in turn, means that an investor who may be using the products of an investment manager have to be realistic about the manager's individual claims because to beat the market averages he has to be right much more often than 50 per cent of the time. Sometimes a manager might need to aim at 75 per cent success, which becomes a stiff test. And this is quite apart from the inevitable costs involved in switching around the mix of shares or assets in the portfolio.

So investors need to be careful about trying to pick the best active investment managers. The best that managers can hope to achieve (and claim in advertisements) is a consistent performance over a period, or a style which aims to produce an average or above-average return while limiting risks to acceptable levels.

Investors in retail products also need to shop carefully for managed equity funds which may have slightly different aims. Some, for instance, emphasise better, fully franked income; others may aim mainly for capital growth, concentrate on a small number of leading stocks, lean towards smaller companies, or emphasise avoiding risks.

THE BOTTOM-UP APPROACH

The alternative approach to the top-down style is the bottom-up approach. This is usually associated with investment managers who have a distinctive philosophy and a disciplined approach to selecting investments. This applies mostly to share portfolios, although it can occasionally be adapted to balanced portfolios containing a variety of asset classes.

Two of the world's best-known bottom-up share investors have histories which go back to the 1940s — the Fidelity group founded by Edward C Johnson and the Templeton group, founded by Sir John Templeton. Both
founders based their approach on finding shares which
offer fundamental value and buying only these stocks.
Their approach is that it does not necessarily matter which
industry the company is in or the geographical mix which
results, as long as the investments offer value.

Fidelity's mission statement says its investment approach
basically aims to identify fundamental value because, by
this method, it reduces considerably the risk to an investor
of long-term loss and also produces superior longer-term
returns. The group does not automatically select well-
known companies; indeed many of its shares are among
the lesser-known companies. Peter Lynch, the man who
turned the Fidelity Magellan Fund into such a winner, says
in his book *One Up on Wall Street* (Simon and Schuster)
that no one in Fidelity ever told him the fund must own
Xerox. As a result, Lynch sought out winners among stocks
like La Quinta Motor Inns or Dunkin' Donuts.

Then again, Fidelity was always going to be different
from the general run of investment managers because of
the influence of its founder, Edward Johnson II — always
called Mr Johnson, both by his staff and by his competitors. Mr Johnson believed that you invested in shares not
to preserve capital but to make money, says Lynch. Then
you take your profits and invest in more stocks. 'Stocks you
trade; it's wives you're stuck with,' said Mr Johnson.

That sort of talk would be unlikely to have come from
Sir John Templeton, the God-fearing founder of another
renowned stock-picking investment management group
which bears his name. He has been in his investment business since 1937 and the group he runs has had a record of
outperforming the market over most of its 40-plus years of
public operation. Sir John, born on a farm in Tennessee,
now lives in the Bahamas and his group now runs major
US and international funds.

Templeton is also driven by research aimed at identifying value investments which are bargain-priced. Sir John
defines the group's task this way: 'The first duty of a security analyst is to discover investment opportunities that

result in superior total real returns, net after tax, for his client.'

As an example of that concentration, the Templeton group identified Australian bank shares as among the best value around the world in the 1980s and, like the Adelaide Steamship's John Spalvins, bought large holdings at the start of their bull run.

Templeton's decision to be headquartered in the Bahamas rather than in Wall Street in New York seems to work. Templeton says simply: 'If you are going to produce a better record than other people, you must not buy the same things as they . . . and when you are a thousand miles away in a different nation, it's easier to buy the things that other people are selling and to sell the things that other people are buying.'

Warren Buffett, who started in investment the same time as Templeton, also follows this policy. He operates out of Omaha, Nebraska, which is hardly a major financial centre. He says that he gets all the mail, information and facts he needs in Omaha. 'And, unlike Wall Street, you'll notice we don't have 50 people coming up and whispering in our ear that we should be doing this or that this afternoon. I like the lack of stimulation. Here, we get facts not stimulation.'

As these views might suggest, the bottom-up stock pickers can sometimes be idiosyncratic operators. They don't bother so much with economic analysis, asset allocation and balancing volatility with returns; they just buy stocks that their research indicates are bargains.

Both Templeton and Fidelity sell retail international funds in Australia and Templeton has an Australian listed fund. Of the local investment managers, Rothschild Australia operates a 'value' approach in its equity portfolios which offers a modified local version of this type of operation, while in the managed equity funds, Advance Imputation Fund, Perpetual Trustees and the AMP Imputation Trust all tend towards fundamental value or relative value methods.

You might think that the stock pickers or bottom-up investors would turn out to be more short-term traders while the top-down operators tend to be longer-term holders, but this is not necessarily true. Templeton certainly takes a long-term view, as does Fidelity. Warren Buffett says he believes that if you are making a good investment you should not be concerned even if the stock market were closed for several years.

Value investors and bottom-up operators sometimes need a longer period to establish a record and Templeton, in particular, does not believe in trading stocks. Few of these managers outperform the market indices regularly each year and yet, over a long period, they produce much better results.

This means that they produce very strong outperformance when they do better, often after spending several years languishing behind the indices, perhaps because they have been following their own selections instead of the current fashions. In short, those who use a bottom-up approach need to be patient and prepared to ignore current investment fashion.

In Australia in the six years since the 1987 stock market collapse most investment managers have stuck to top-down asset allocation methods. Yet the best performances in wholesale managed funds has come from BT Australia and Maple-Brown Abbott with bottom-up, active management approach.

Most of the managers have been performing as active managers who have run balanced portfolios moderately weighted towards shares and concentrated in 20 or 30 of the major stocks. Everyone — large local managers, small individual investors and overseas investors — has been concentrating on the major stocks. As a result, the weight of money has virtually guaranteed reasonable performance.

THE OPTIONS MARKETS

Some of this concentration in major stocks reflects the need to be conservative and to avoid capital losses, as occurred with the shares of the high-fliers of the mid-1980s. Some of it was a result of the pursuit of fully franked dividends from 1985–86 onwards. But, as more and more investment managers became users of the options markets to hedge their portfolio positions, the concentration on these major stocks mainly reflected the fact that the options markets were an available alternative.

The importance of the options markets in determining major trends on the stock exchange should not be underestimated. The use of options allows the large investors to deal in very large parcels of shares relatively easily since each option contract involves 1000 shares of the underlying share. This means that large institutions which want to change their portfolios quickly can do so via the options markets. The big investors can also hedge their positions via options so that they can insure against a fall in share prices or get set to benefit from a rise in prices.

Several major investment groups now operate sophisticated strategies which depend on options trading. These strategies are framed in such a way that the portfolio has very little risk of falling, a result achieved by using a combination of options which provides the limit on the downside at the expense of losing some of the gains which a normal portfolio of shares, rather than options, might achieve. The use of these strategies has been embraced in 'protected' funds by several of the mainstream managers, including ANZ Funds Management, BT Australia, County Nat-West, Macquarie and Westpac Investment Management.

Because of the concentration of funds invested in the same 20 or 30 major companies and the fairly widespread use of similar options trading strategies, there is a tendency for many of the major managers' results to become similar. This is the inevitable proof of Sir John Templeton's view: if you want average results, invest in what everyone other manager is buying.

THE DECISION-MAKERS

The investment managers argue that they are largely forced into this approach by the so-called 'short-termism' which rules the investment management world. The trustees of large superannuation funds, it is claimed, are too obsessed with month-by-month relative performance and tend to hire or fire investment managers based largely on short-term results.

Several firms of actuaries produce quarterly 'league tables' of investment managers who are handling about $40 billion of pooled superannuation fund money (and a lot more of individually operated portfolios). Two or three actuaries produce monthly figures, though not all of them report for periods shorter than three months. Other actuaries produce surveys of performances on a quarterly basis.

While there is always competition for new funds to manage, no-one forces investment managers to slavishly follow the herd or try to score coups with risky market timing. The fact is that consistent, rather than spectacular, performance is what most superannuation fund trustees are seeking. As well, many funds hire actuaries as investment consultants to help in the choice of managers of the fund's money, so the consultants have a major input into the choice of manager.

Increasingly among the larger superannuation funds there is much less reliance on performance alone and the 'beauty parades' (the selection process of new investment managers for a fund). Trustees usually concentrate more on the management attributes of prospective fund managers. More and more, investment managers have to perform according to a superannuation fund's mandate, rather than do their own thing, so compatibility between trustees' wishes and the manager's style is one of the most important attributes.

Slowly, we are seeing the development of a complex system of managing the rapidly increasing number of superannuation funds. Under the present system of trustees taking responsibility for the funds, the final decision rests with the trustees, but there is a growing number of people who have some input into the decision.

First, there are the investment experts at the actuarial firms, who measure performance and risk and, using computers, can determine the optimum policy for a given range of desired return/risk profiles. The actuarial consultants often frame proposals for trustees, advise them on potential managers of the funds and interpret the performance figures. In addition, the actuaries separately assess whether the fund's combination of contributions and investment returns is likely to result in a deficit or a surplus after taking into account its current and potential liabilities to members of the funds.

Second, the investment managers themselves regularly consult with the superannuation fund trustees, either individually or at regular group briefings. The managers are always experimenting and refining their investment strategies and techniques. Any breakthroughs are usually copied quickly (if they appear to work) or subtly condemned (if they appear to be less than well-founded). There is a lot of interchange of ideas and staff between the consultants and the actual investment managers.

Third, the major stockbroking and investment banking groups provide a huge amount of research information to the investment managers and the trustees of funds. This can range from grassroots research based on the analysis of accounts and a visit to a company's plant to sophisticated models of portfolio strategies or complex options-trading techniques designed to produce particular outcomes (such as hedging against rises or falls in interest rates).

Fourth, the trustees themselves have to sift much of this information and apply what in the US is called 'the prudent man' test because they, as trustees, are personally responsible to their members for their decisions. This responsibility is becoming recognised more widely in the current climate where the government and regulators are, rightly, increasing their scrutiny of superannuation funds.

Finally, there is much greater input into the management and investment decisions of superannuation funds from the actual members of funds. Most major funds now have employee trustees, whether nominated or elected. In the major industry funds there is regular interchange between the members and trustees. Communication with members is now regarded as a very important part of the trustees' job. Members of individual funds are much more able (and likely) to lobby their trustees.

As well, there has been an upsurge in the number of outside people with ideas on how superannuation funds should invest. This is not necessarily regarded as a good thing by the superannuation industry and investment managers generally — they regard it as unwarranted interference by do-gooders — but it is part of a growing public debate on how major savings-collecting institutions should behave and invest, which is injecting a new burst of democracy into the investment management business.

5

THE RULES OF THE GAME

It is possible that the stock exchange fraternity is, for reasons unknown, disguising its gigantic intellect, but it is more likely that some other forces are at work. Our guess is that there is some sort of "invisible hand" guiding the individuals concerned (mostly against their own better judgement) into the correct path.

— *Roger Nightingale, circular from stockbrokers Smith New Court (London), January 1991*

*T*here may be almost as many investment rules as there are investment choices. In presenting some as guidance, this book does not intend to ram a list of Ten Commandments down the necks of readers. But we will look at Ten Rules which seem to have worked in the past and see how they can help most investors.

The higher the return, the higher the risk.   *RULE 1*

This rule should be ingrained in every investor's mind and is as basic as the law of gravity for scientists. Like the law of gravity it has never been repealed, despite what some people will tell investors when selling them a dubious investment — and despite what some investors tell themselves when in the grip of boom-time delusions. But, as we noted earlier, the real essence of investing is to understand the trade-off between risk and return and to produce the best and most appropriate investment mix. For an elderly widow this might be the safety of bank deposits; for a young person it might be growth-oriented shares.

When the investment experts speak about risk, they are usually referring to the volatility of returns in various sorts of investments. This relates to one part of investment risk — the possibility that sometimes there may be no return or a lower return than expected. Anyone who invests in shares has to accept this possibility since dividends on shares are not automatic.

There also is the second part of risk: the possibility that you may not get back all of your original capital or that, when you want to sell, it may be worth less than your purchase price. People investing for relatively short periods of time — say three years or less — should apply the test of security to the investment alternatives. This says simply that sometimes return of the capital is more important than the return on the capital. Once again, this happens more often with shares, although there are always cases like Pyramid or Estate Mortgage (not to mention other finance and land group failures in the 1960s) in which investors lose some of their capital invested in fixed interest deposits or debentures.

To understand risk properly, we need to describe it more precisely. There are, in fact, three types of investment risk:

1. **The general market risk** relates to a greater or lesser extent to all stocks and most investments. This risk depends on overall economic conditions.

2. **Market segment risk** relates to a particular segment of the share market — say, that mining shares will perform poorly relative to industrial shares or that bank shares will do much better than retail shares.

3. **Specific risk** relates to the performance of a particular share in an investment portfolio.

The first, general market risk, is the one which is hardest to control, short of having most of a portfolio in short-term cash holdings in times of recession. Note that we are now talking about 'controlling risk' rather than eliminating risk. The only guaranteed way to eliminate risk completely is not to invest at all. But investing sensibly over long periods goes as close as possible to eliminating most of the risk, as we will see when we consider the long-term record.

The market segment risk can be handled by a careful study of the likely economic scene and forecasts which will, hopefully, identify the possible winners and losers. For instance, if you believed that the Australian dollar was most likely to depreciate against the $US, you might put money into US shares or concentrate more funds in the shares of overseas mineral exporters which are paid in $US and which would gain from a devaluation.

The specific risk of one investment not performing as planned can only be overcome by careful investigation before buying and regular checks on the performance of the shares and of the company after buying.

It also can be worth remembering that, in times like 1990 when interest rates were declining but the economy was sliding into recession, there were specific risks that individual companies might suffer from the recession's effects. For investors seeking an investment which could benefit from falling interest rates, bonds might have made more sense in this relatively brief period because the specific company risk is not present.

We will look again at the three types of risk in the next chapter.

Investors should seek to invest their capital safely and to earn a reasonable return.   *RULE 2*

This rule is largely a paraphrase of a definition given in the 1930s by Benjamin Graham (the man generally acknowledged as the father of modern investment analysis) but it is worth considering even in the 1990s. In effect, it rules out as 'investments' such things as owning your own home (there is no return — apart from the rent you don't have to pay), gold, works of art and other collectables. It certainly rules out speculation in non-dividend paying shares or punting on the horses, Lotto numbers or poker machines.

At this point, we need to consider what is a reasonable rate of return since all things in investment, as in life, are relative. The professional managers often talk about a benchmark. Benchmarks in professional investment generally are the widely accepted market indices (such as the Dow Jones or Standard & Poors indices in the US, or the all ordinaries in Australia). The managers also talk about a 'real' return. This, quite simply, is the amount by which a return exceeds the current level of inflation.

In other words, we are making inflation (or its downside, the depreciation in the purchasing power of the currency) our benchmark. Most serious investors want at least to maintain the purchasing power of their capital and, if possible increase it. Therefore, earning a real rate of interest becomes an essential target.

RULE 3   **Remember the difference between price and value.**

It was Oscar Wilde who said, 'A cynic knows the price of everything and the value of nothing.' He would have been able to observe plenty of cynics in the stock market, since the day-to-day traders and dealers, not to mention many of the professional managers, are interested only in the market price of a share.

For those people in daily, close contact with the physical stock market, a 'buy' on the market is a share which is rising while a 'sell' is one which is falling. If they are not sure which way the stock will move, then they undertake options strategies which, in effect, give them an each-way bet.

This is not the best strategy for the small operator, nor is it the approach for a true investor. Instead, true investors ought to be thankful for the emphasis on short-term trading and on share prices by the professional operators. This makes it that much easier for the investor to concentrate on the value of a share rather than its price.

RULE 4   **Buy cheap and sell dear.**

This rule was first attributed to Myer Rothschild, the founder of the House of Rothschild. It can be approached as an intellectual challenge to identify cheap shares and buy them before the rest of the market realises and to sell shares when they appear to be overvalued. Many investors and analysts at investment institutions and stockbroking firms spend much of their time on these activities. As a result, with their efforts concentrated on a few dozen stocks, the market in the most actively traded stocks tends not to run to large over- or under-valuations.

Most of the major investment managers and many of the large stockbrokers now have highly developed models which attempt to rate the relative value of the share market generally and share prices in individual companies. Individual investors may find these too complex, even if they have access to them.

For most investors, however, use of the 'buy low; sell high' rule in its several variations will often keep them on the right path in assessing shares and avoiding the excessive concentration on the price of a share rather than on its value. In general, these rules are summed up by the advice to 'buy too early and sell too soon'. In other words, in the words of one American investment guru, Martin Zweig, 'beware of the crowd'.

An interest in psychology does not go astray in the investment markets. There is a lot of emphasis on the way that the stock market behaves as does an irrational crowd. Several experts have gone back to the first work on the psychology of crowds by Dr Gustave Le Bon written almost 100 years ago. He first put his finger on the concept of a psychological crowd — for instance, all those people speculating in a stock market — which makes people feel, think and act in a way quite different to their normal behaviour.

Be disciplined. *RULE 5*

This rule covers both the way investors approach the analysis of investments and, in particular, the actual buying and selling of shares.

The stock market, in most of its moods, can distract investors from the main task of analysing shares and trying to buy cheap and sell dear. Exposure to the widespread pessimism in a bear market can distract investors and cause them to hesitate. At the opposite extreme, the excitement of a bull market can cause a rush of blood to the head of even the most experienced investor.

The story of long-term investors who miss out on big killings in a roaring bull market are legion. A cautious investor wants to buy a share because of a belief in the worth of the stock, but in a boom market the basic reason for buying a share is the near-certainty that it will rise in price the next moment. In these circumstances, it is essential for investors to resist the temptation to act on impulse.

Know what you are buying. *RULE 6*

It is not enough to buy a share because (a) your stockbroker recommends it; (b) it has a high yield and a low price/earnings ratio; or even (c) that you like its name. The truly serious investor should know his shares intimately.

A couple of years ago, I met an elderly shareholder in a leading Melbourne-based company at an annual meeting and we got talking. I asked him how much he had lost in the 1987 collapse. 'Hardly anything,' he replied. I asked him the secret of his success in picking companies which did not collapse.

'It's simple,' he said. 'I never buy shares in companies if I can't see where they have earned their profit and I don't buy shares in companies where I can't understand the accounts.'

The need to be informed is even more important when people are buying managed investment products. In the 1987 collapse, there were countless people who were horrified when the value of their rollover funds dropped sharply. They claimed they had not been told by their advisers that the rollover funds were, in many cases, quite heavily invested in the booming stock market. (Just how these investors imagined their rollover investments had been achieving annual earning rates of 30 to 40 per cent without an exposure to the stock market is not clear.)

Similarly, many people who bought insurance bonds did not realise that the name 'bond' was a misnomer and that they really owned a single premium insurance policy which had its surrender value linked directly to market prices in the bond market and, more significantly, in the property and share markets.

Finally, many investors who sought a higher than normal fixed interest return in mortgage trusts operated by Estate Mortgage appeared to believe the television advertising line, 'Nice and safe', and other slogans which suggested that the investment was just like a bank, only better. Few people took the trouble to read the prospectus or to investigate where the mortgage funds were being lent.

RULE 7 **Be flexible.**

US investment expert Martin Zweig has four rules for investors; the first is to beware of the crowd and the second is to be flexible. He tells investors and fellow funds managers that 'it's okay to be wrong, but it's unforgivable to stay wrong'. This relates particularly to those investment managers who are attempting to beat the crowd in the market-timing stakes and stay too long in shares, or who miss the rally in specific markets such as bonds.

His final two rules are not to fight the central bank (in the case of the US, the Federal Reserve Board, or in Australia, the Reserve Bank of Australia) and 'don't fight the tape', the American way of saying to go with the market.

For true investors, the rule of not battling against the central bank's monetary policy is sensible. There is a clear connection between the growth in the supply of money and the stock market, since a plentiful supply of money assures investors (and speculators) of fuel for a boom market. Similarly, when the monetary authorities start to tighten credit and increase interest rates, most investors will heed the warning signs.

Make assumptions, but do not treat them as certainties. *RULE 8*

This is an extension of the seventh rule but it is worth a place on its own merits.

Those people who reasoned that gold prices would rise in 1990 because of the Gulf crisis came horribly unstuck, even though the crisis and the subsequent war produced the sort of scenario which gold buffs love — instability, then a shooting war in the Middle East and a threat to oil production. Instead, oil stayed in oversupply, oil prices fell rather than rose when the shooting started and the rush of speculative funds seeking certainty in uncertain times went into the American dollar instead of gold bars.

Even if investors are confident of their assumptions and theories, they should re-test them regularly and monitor the progress of a company or a share. Whether investors are running with the herd or taking a view contrary to the general opinion, they should always have an escape route or at least ask themselves, 'What happens if I'm wrong?'

Fortunes can be made on the basis of bold investments but fortunes can also be lost when investors fail to realise that they have overreached themselves.

Never forget that liquidity of an investment is para- *RULE 9*
mount.

Investors in many unlisted property trusts and mortgage trusts forgot this simple rule. Mind you, they were given plenty of encouragement to do so, since the prospectuses, managers and advisers all told them that they could redeem their funds after giving specified notice of a month or so.

What they forgot was that such a trust (unless it had the large resources of a rich parent company) cannot promise investors such liquidity if it cannot be sure of at least something like the same underlying liquidity in its own assets. Once cash flowing in dries up, there is only one way a property trust can meet redemptions and that is to sell off part of its assets.

Property trust investors forgot about liquidity because they had closed their eyes to the most liquid of all markets — the share market. They had rushed into unlisted property trusts to avoid the ups and downs of share prices, forgetting that the volatility of daily prices was the price investors paid for immediate liquidity.

They also fell into the trap of believing in fairies at the bottom of the garden: that they could count on redemption at net asset value even though the stock market and everyday experience was telling them that property values generally were declining and that redemptions at above-market levels could only continue for a limited time.

RULE 10 **Never forget that you are dealing with markets and that markets are driven by only two emotions — fear and greed.**

If investors make one regular mistake, it is to forget that people make up the markets. People get caught up in the boom fever and pay silly prices for worthless shares. In bear markets, people get carried away with the ruling pessimism and are over-eager to believe the worst rumours. Greed drives bull markets and fear dominates bear markets and these can be two of the most powerful human emotions.

Investors probably need to make a mistake or two in boom and bear markets before they learn these lessons. Books can list all the dangers but most people generally learn the hard lessons best by personal experience.

Some people apply simple rules like 'never go back to a stock for a second helping'. I can relate to this rule because of an experience in Australian Oil & Gas (AOG) in the early 1960s. I had bought the shares for about $1.30 in anticipation of an oil find at one drill site, only to see this well fail and the shares fall, but then jump to $10 after oil was found at a second attempt at the Moonie field in south-eastern Queensland.

Despite holding the shares by accident — and at a paper loss after the first drilling failure — I was able to sell at a handsome profit. Not content with that, when AOG announced a rights issue, I bought the rights as a lower-priced speculation on the current exploration well. By then, AOG had had its rise, the speculators had sold and the investors had begun to buy. I lost money on the rights but more importantly, I learned that there was more luck than good judgement in speculating in oil shares.

6

THE RISKS

What we anticipate seldom occurs. What we least expect generally happens.

— Benjamin Disraeli

So much for the Ten Rules of investment — and there are probably many more — but there is really only one test of an investment approach: the sleep test.

No matter how well designed, no investment approach is a good one if you cannot sleep at night. (The only exception to this rule would be those speculators who have become addicted to gambling on the American futures exchange and who have to stay up all night in Australia to trade during the US trading hours.) In other words, tailor the risks in your investments to the risks you as a person are prepared to take.

Some people are inveterate worriers. They always seem to know someone who has lost money in a poor investment or, even without first-hand experience, they can imagine the worst about any investment. The cause of worry or anxiety is often inexperience or a lack of knowledge of the investment or a lack of knowledge of the way the investment world operates.

These people need reassurance and the appropriate knowledge. Since investment is often a do-it-yourself exercise, this may not be easy. At the very least, however, those investors feeling their way need someone with whom they can share concerns and seek reassurance. Sometimes this may be a friend or a relative; often it will be their investment adviser, whether a stockbroker, financial planner or adviser, accountant or solicitor.

At the other extreme, some people can adopt a devil-may-care approach to investment and neglect to ask the obvious questions or to take the most rudimentary precautions. There is plenty of evidence that confidence tricksters find it easier to relieve people of money using an investment scam than using most other recognised methods.

Slick-talking international con men got several million dollars from Australian investors in the mid-1980s simply by selling them shares over the telephone. The victims were not ordinary people caught by door-to-door salesmen but well-off investors gleaned from the share registry of large Australian companies who had replied to a junk mail offer of a free investment newsletter.

After three months of softening up via newsletters which, along with legitimate international shares, always featured one bogus share which continued to rise in price, the con men would ring their victims from Europe. Basically, they were asking people to buy about $5000 of what turned out to be 1 cent shares in a Liechtenstein company formed by an obscure investment bank for a far from prosperous British computer software company. You were not told that, of course; instead the North American accent extolled the virtues of the stock and offered investors the chance to get in before the stock was listed.

The sales pitch was so slick that many Australian investors forgot to ask the obvious questions like: 'Where are the shares being listed?' and 'Can I see a prospectus and a balance sheet?' Not to mention the more obvious question: how do you trust someone from a broking firm you've never heard of, who tries to sell you shares over the telephone in a company which you've no proof even exists?

Although it might seem harsh, perhaps the only way people will learn to exercise a little more care is for them to lose money as a result of their own carelessness. Experience is a great teacher, as long as the victims learn the lesson and recognise the risks which lurk behind the sales pitch.

The problem, however, is that whenever a large number of people lose money from the failure of a large, well-known organisation, a great cry goes up from the public: 'They ought to do something about it.'

PROTECTIVE LEGISLATION

Well, 'they' (the Federal Government) have done something. They have introduced national corporations legislation which requires a prospectus virtually every time shares or securities are issued to the public. Previously, there were cumbersome definitions of which types of investment required a prospectus and which did not. But now the law is clear: all issues to the public require a prospectus, except for shares issued to large, professional investors, who are excluded under the big and ugly rule — that they are assumed to be big enough and ugly enough to look after themselves.

Most corporate and investment law has two objectives: to make it possible to catch and punish wrongdoers and to provide assurance to investors generally that they are being protected; in other words, to remove from the markets the fear of old-fashioned crookedness. There is more than a slight problem, however, when the law fails to catch, convict and punish obvious wrongdoing: investors lose faith in the system, as we saw in the aftermath of the collapse of the 1980s boom. This is why everyone in the investment world still hopes that the combination of the new legislation and a new watchdog, the Australian Securities Commission, with bite as well as bark, will redress the problems.

But there is an old adage in the business world: you cannot legislate for honesty. For some corporate operators, the existence of a law is only an incentive to find a way around or through the provisions. No investor should assume that the new corporate law and an upgraded regulatory system can provide complete protection.

The corollary is that in times of boom when greed takes over it is almost impossible to protect people from their own foolishness. The new laws try to do so, by requiring companies, directors and promoters to give all the information necessary for investors — and then providing the means for those who lose money to sue anyone who signed a prospectus. This means that stockbrokers, the company directors, the investigating accountants and auditors, any other experts and the lawyers can all be sued by investors. The cynics say this is simply providing a large enough population of potential targets that, after the collapse, disgruntled investors have a chance of finding someone with some money left who can be sued for damages.

It is far better, of course, for investors to avoid bad investments in the first place because even if they may manage to extract damages after long legal battles this will be no compensation for the initial loss and the time which will be involved — as, for example, in the long battles ahead of those who lent money to Estate Mortgage.

The other problem in Australia has been the general lack of litigation by investors who lost money against the people who advised them. Most of the actions for damages have been against auditors and a number of people believe that if there had been a few more damages suits against bad advice then some of the cavalier advice by some advisers would have been avoided.

THE THREE TYPES OF RISK

In grappling with the way to apply our 'sleep test' to an investment approach, we need to go back to that explanation in Chapter 5 of the different sorts of risk — general market risk, market segment risk and specific risk. Investors may need to take different action to cope with these different risks.

Take the general market risk: if people are genuinely concerned that the economic situation overall is going to be so poor that most investments look risky, then they clearly need to concentrate on leaving their savings on deposit or in near-cash deposits with governments or banks. But, before they take this approach, investors ought to get a second opinion on whether the general economic outlook is bad enough to justify such a blanket condemnation of any investment other than cash on deposit.

The market segment risk probably provides more specific worries for investors. They are concerned that the share market may go down rather than up; they fear that they may tie up funds in fixed interest securities for long terms and then see interest rates rise. The obvious solutions to these risk worries are to seek advice and analysis on the specific market segments, or to diversify an invest-

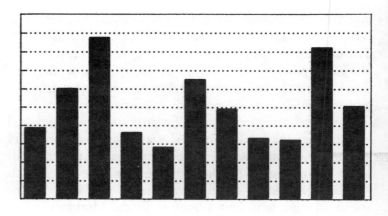

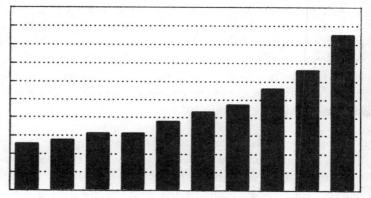

ment portfolio sufficiently to hope that these factors cancel each other out in the long term.

The third worry of specific risk — that is, the company whose shares you buy turns out to be a laggard in market performance or produces no income and falls in value — probably puts the greatest pressure on individual investors. This is where a new investor needs to tread cautiously.

To handle specific risks, investors can either avoid the risk completely or try to minimise the risk. The only way to avoid the risk of selecting a poor share investment is either to buy government bonds or debentures or leave the money in cash. To minimise the risk, people need to research their investments carefully and then to spread their funds in a range of investments to diversify their risk. Even then, incidentally, there can be varying returns. For instance, consider the two graphs shown above. Which one looks more volatile and risky?

INTEREST RATE VOLATILITY

90 DAY BILL YIELDS AT JUNE 30

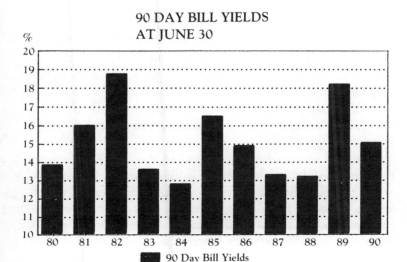

90 Day Bill Yields

PACIFIC DUNLOP
GROWTH IN DIVIDENDS

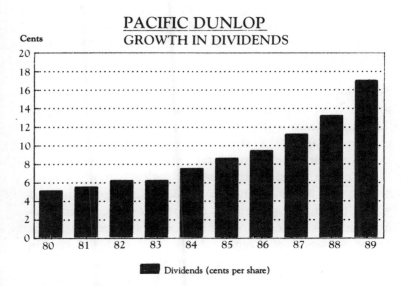

Dividends (cents per share)

Source: Potter Warburg Research

If you nominated the top one as the more risky, what is your reaction when we add the captions and labels to the graphs (see above)?

In fact, the steady, upward growth in income was provided by Pacific Dunlop shares while the varying rates of interest were the result of investing in short-term bank bills.

DIVERSIFICATION IS THE BEST SAFEGUARD

When we really get down to attempting to control specific risks in investments, it usually ends up with a version of the old adage, 'Don't put all your eggs in one basket.' Splitting investment funds between two or more shares is one way of trying to minimise specific risk and all investors should aim to have some diversification in their share portfolio.

There is an alternative version of the adage: 'Put your eggs into one basket but watch it like a hawk.' Or perhaps more realistically, get someone with experience to watch it like a hawk. To do this, investors seek a single investment where the risk is spread among dozens of investments by professional investment managers.

For share market investors, this can be achieved by buying various investment trusts run by a range of investment managers (ranging from banks and life offices to professional fund managers). These can be either listed or unlisted trusts and we look at these two alternatives in more detail later.

PLAYING THE LONG-TERM AVERAGES

So, how does an individual investor manage to find an approach which enables him to sleep peacefully at night? The answer is to look at how the professional investors and managers handle the same sort of risks. Essentially, they play the averages in longer-term investment markets.

First, let's consider the risks of widely varying returns among the best-measured investments, the pooled funds which the major investment managers run for superannuation funds. These performances are monitored by several major actuaries on a regular basis. This is the picture of returns (before charges) from Sedgwick Noble Lowndes for the 1993 calendar year:

Median, all managers .... +26.0%
Best performer .... +34.0%
Worst performer .... +18.1%

Clearly, selecting the best manager on those yearly figures would be a lottery. In fact, in some annual surveys, sometimes the worst performer in one year became the best performer the next year.

But, now let's look at the results for the five years to 1993:

Median return all managers .... +13.1%
Best performer .... +15.8%
Worst performer .... +9.5%

Notice how the range of performances has narrowed to within 2.7 per cent on the upside and 3.6 per cent on the downside. And remember how, in Chapter 1, the actuaries' figures showed how the chances of losses lessened with time. A longer, ten-year period would be a reasonable time over which to judge an investment manager, since it will probably cover a complete cycle in the investment market from boom to bust and sometimes back again. The 10 year figures show a median return of 14.7 per cent, with the best return 16.9 per cent and the worst 11.7 per cent.

It could be argued, of course, that since an index of all maturities of Commonwealth bonds returned more than 15 per cent compound a year for the ten years, the investment managers were not exactly setting the world on fire with their performance. Their portfolios comprised a mix of various investment assets but they generally offered a higher risk than bonds. But still, that higher risk in the managers' portfolios had achieved a strong outperformance over the key inflation measures, confirming that if we accept a higher risk we can achieve a higher return.

The rate of inflation shown by the Consumer Price Index in the ten years to 1993 was 5.3 per cent, so even the worst-performing manager improved on that by a substantial margin. For superannuation funds (whose long-term liabilities rise in line with wages and salaries), the key benchmark is really the rate of growth in average earnings. At 6.0 per cent a year in the ten years, this also was beaten comfortably even by the worst-performing manager.

In other words, the other major risk — the risk of investments not keeping pace with inflation — has been overcome, within what would appear to be an acceptable range of best/worst performances over a significant time period.

For the smaller investor, the message is fairly simple: the

risks of widely varying returns can be reduced sharply by a diversified portfolio and the ups and downs in performance will be smoothed out over a period of time.

That's the theory. How do you do it? Basically, by playing the long-term averages. The real choice is whether you do it yourself or pay an investment manager to do it for you.

7

THE RETURNS

A large proportion of our positive activities depend on spontaneous optimism rather than on mathematical expectation...Most, probably, of our decisions to do something positive...can only be taken as a result of animal spirits...

— *John Maynard Keynes on how investors' long-term expectations operate*

*A*s a general rule, the investment world's bookies, the actuaries, count on returns in the long term of around ten per cent. This is a rough rule of thumb and it is before allowing for inflation or for tax. In fact, the long-term 'real' returns (after taking inflation out of the earning rates) is probably around five per cent but it could vary to as low as two per cent.

The main problem with counting on those long-term returns is that, as John Maynard Keynes remarked, in the long run we are all dead. And it is all very well to have expectations as long as we realise, as Disraeli remarked: 'What we anticipate seldom occurs; what we least expect generally happens.' Traditionally, the only investors who could take a very long-term view were the life assurance companies, investing people's savings in many cases for their entire lifetime. More recently, superannuation funds, investing people's savings during a 30- or 40-year working lifetime, have become the more usual long-term investors.

But these days even the traditional life offices and managers of superannuation fund investments have been forced to concentrate on much shorter time periods. They have to prove their skills to investors over 3- and 12-month periods, and a 5-year period is probably their long-term time horizon — if the client's patience lasts that long. This means that they are usually forced to supercharge their investments by working their portfolios hard, switching from one stock to another, fiddling with adjustments to percentage holdings and hedging using options, futures and warrants. The reason for this is that of about 50 major investment managers whose investment performances are regularly surveyed, everyone wants to be in the top 10 or 12 performers and everyone wants at least to beat the average return. Arithmetic beats the majority of them, but in the process the investment management game resembles the churning waters at the start of a major swimming race. (To be fair to the major managers, however, it is worth noting that despite the criticism of 'short-termism' by investment managers over the last decade they have produced returns averaging around 15 per cent a year.)

The ordinary investor, standing on the shores of investment, cannot be blamed for not wanting to dive into these boiling waters. Not only does the savage competition between investment managers deter direct investment, but it must also cause investors to worry about picking the wrong manager.

Even the managers charging the highest fees (based either on past performance or purely on what the market will bear) do not necessarily provide the highest returns. Several boom-time managers of superannuation money have gone completely out of business; others exist with only a few million dollars of funds under management. Nor, for that matter, is the best-performing fund necessarily the one drawing the most money into it. Reputation (from past years' performance) and the resources devoted to selling the product appear to play an important part in the actual size of funds.

Investors in retail investment products have had good cause for concern because inept management has lost large amounts of investors' funds, and it is not just fringe operators who are to blame. In fact, the average performance over the three years to the end of 1990 by equity trusts aiming for capital growth was the loss of about a fifth of investors' initial stake. With a much better year in 1991, the average share growth fund produced a small improvement for the three years to 1991 but this was at a compound rate of growth of only 4.5 per cent, only half the return achieved on the all ordinaries accumulation index.

But there are at least a dozen managers which have managed to outperform the stock market averages over the last three years with their trusts which they sell to retail investors. Most financial advisers should be able to discover these but, based on the widely-used figures produced by ASSIRT, a major funds management researcher, these managers mainstream equity trusts (excluding gold and resources trusts) beat the market average growth of 14.9 per cent over the three years to March 1993: AFT*, AMP, BT Australia, First State*, Global*, GT, HSBC (formerly Wardley), Jardine Fleming, Mercantile Mutual, National Mutual*, Oceanic, Perpetual Trustees, Potter Warburg, Rothschild, Schroder and Tyndall*. (The managers are listed alphabetically; * indicates the manager had more than one individual trust which beat the stock market average.)

In general, the large investment managers produce much the same results in their retail funds as they do in the wholesale market aimed at superannuation fund clients. Four of the better-performing managers of retail equity trusts also crop up in the list of the best-performing investment managers for superannuation fund money.

This is how the large wholesale superannuation fund managers rank, based on performances over the ten years to December 1993:

Manager	Return % p.a.	Rank
Mercantile Mutual	16.9	1
BTA Retirement	16.2	2
MLC Growth	15.7	3
National Mutual FM	15.1	4
Prudential	15.1	5
Zurich	15.0	6
Legal & General	14.8	7
Westpac Group	14.8	8
Rothschild	14.7	9
Suncorp Balanced	14.4	10

Source: Sedwick Noble Lowndes

So, the initial message for investors who are considering

MANAGER PERFORMANCES

an investment manager to run their funds is that you can get reasonable performance — even above-average performance — if you look carefully and if you are prepared to pay for it.

Just as investors need to weigh risk versus returns, so they also need to weigh the returns achieved against the costs charged.

Most managed investments in the equity area charge an entry fee of between four and six per cent. This often goes to the financial adviser or stockbroker but investors should haggle with the manager or the adviser to get a rebate of part of this fee. Then there are management fees, trustee fees and reimbursement of some expenses of running the trust. Most prospectuses now show this as a 'management expense ratio' and express it as a percentage of the issue price of the unit. These management expense ratios can range from 0.5 to more than three per cent — double the fees on wholesale funds — and there will almost certainly be pressure on fund managers to reduce these costs on retail funds.

The bottom line for investors, then, is that they could be charged up to nine per cent if they are not careful. Even if, as part of the service, investment managers do some of your housekeeping and account-keeping for tax purposes, this is expensive investment management. A stockbroker usually charges a maximum of 2.5 per cent and large investors like superannuation funds may pay only 1 or 1.5 per cent to the managers of pooled superannuation funds. There may still be a fee or commission charged by the financial adviser on top of these charges. However, these days, investors would be wise to ask for possible rebates of many commissions.

This is expensive investing and even taking average returns over the last decade, it would take more than a year simply for the investor to break even.

When it comes to investment products sold by life insurance companies, the fees in the past were not readily disclosed in the sales promotion brochures, but any deal involving a life insurance salesman (even if he is called an investment adviser) will see commissions payable which will affect your initial investment. So potential customers should look for disclosure of fees and commissions, now required from 1994 onwards.

Brokerage charges by stockbrokers may not look cheap, but they are much cheaper than the fee structures of investment managers. Apart from minimum brokerage charges (which can be $70 to $100), brokers charge about 2.5 per cent on amounts up to $5000, plus stamp duty of 0.3 per cent. Assuming the charges are spread over a three-year period, an investor using a managed product still can be paying at least twice the level of commissions and charges of someone using a stockbroker.

Stockbrokers' charges are called brokerage and not commission for the simple reason that advisers in brokers' offices dealing with individual clients are not usually paid a commission based on individual revenue, unlike some financial advisers and life office agents. From the viewpoint of customers, the moment you see or suspect commission will be paid to the person advising you, take a little longer to check the charges because, in most cases, the commission will come out of your investment funds, one way or another.

My personal view is that many investors can do as well managing their own funds as the average funds manager. This will not be the choice of all investors; indeed, the growth of investment funds into managed investment products in the last few years suggests a majority of people are moving towards managed products. If people want to pay extra for peace of mind and freedom from the hassles of managing a simple investment portfolio, then let them. But everyone should consider at least one direct share investment before they dismiss the process as too difficult.

It is not necessary to indulge in sophisticated analysis or to have extraordinary investment insights to buy shares and make good returns from them over the long term. Simply by buying a listed investment trust, such as Australian Foundation Investment Co (AFIC), will produce very good returns. Over the last decade, the average annual compound rate of return from AFIC shares has dropped below 19 per cent only once in a five year period. In several five-year periods, the average annual rate of return was above 30 per cent. In the ten years to December 1993, AFIC shares produced an average compound rate of return to investors (dividends and capital gains) of 21.86 per cent, according to the Statex figures. Someone who put $1000 into AFIC shares in December 1983 and took up all the new issues since then would have seen it grow to $7220 by 31 December 1993. More significantly for those who look for income, dividend payments increased each year and have been improved further by the effect of new issues of shares either for cash or in bonus issues. In 1980, AFIC shares offered a yield of 6.9 per cent but, ten years later, the dividend growth had increased that yield to 21.4 per cent.

Remember, when you invest in the stock market, you are looking to play the averages. If you are prepared to look beyond a couple of years, then the basic long-term average performances start working in your favour. Those long-term performances — showing that shares have produced average annual returns of more than ten per cent over the last six decades — should reassure most first-time investors.

Just to remind you, here is a summary of the long-term returns from major investments:

THE VERY LONG-TERM RETURNS
65 YEARS TO 1993

	Actual % p.a.	'Real' % p.a.
Shares	10.8	6.0
Bonds	6.5	1.5

COSTS OF INFLATION AND TAX Finally, we should never forget the main aim of investment — to produce a rate of return which is higher than the rate of inflation so that our savings increase in real terms. No investor, therefore, should forget about inflation. Even if inflation rates are reduced further in Australia in the 1990s, a relatively low five per cent inflation rate can reduce the value of a dollar to 61 cents in ten years and to 38 cents in 20 years.

This means equity investments — that is, shares and property — will always outperform fixed interest investments in the long term. They have an additional advantage under the current capital gains tax legislation: investors who have sold assets at a capital profit are allowed to adjust for the general level of inflation as measured by the Consumer Price Index. In other words, the tax man allows you to match inflation in capital gains, taxing only the extra gains above inflation.

Since 1985 when capital gains from then on became taxable, the CPI has risen about 58 per cent. That means investors in shares or real estate have been generally allowed to have their equity investments increase by that amount without having to pay any capital gains tax if they sell. This puts them well ahead of fixed interest investors. Interest rates generally rise during periods of high inflation, as they did in the early 1980s when lenders finally revolted and demanded and got 'real' returns on fixed interest securities. But, even though those higher interest rates are, in theory, compensation to lenders to make up for inflation, the tax laws do not recognise this and levy tax on all the interest received.

So, in summary, shares and real estate over the long term provide higher returns than bonds and other fixed interest securities. They also have the advantage under current capital gains tax legislation that gains due to inflation are not taxed, giving investors a 'free ride'.

Shares have an additional advantage which we briefly mentioned earlier in the book: many dividends paid by companies offer tax rebates which make the dividends tax free or taxable at a low rate. We will look at these tax advantages of ordinary shares in the next chapter to see how they have changed the whole outlook for individual investors in shares.

8

IMPLICATIONS OF IMPUTATION

Income taxes, especially when they discriminate against 'unearned income', taxes on capital profits, death duties and the like are as relevant as the rate of interest...

— *John Maynard Keynes*

*I*nvesting in shares has changed dramatically since 1985. The reason: the introduction of capital gains tax and dividend imputation.

To those unfamiliar with the jargon of share investment, that basically means that the past rules were turned completely upside down — dividends now are not taxable and capital gains are.

Until the introduction of capital gains tax, in operation since 21 September 1985, most long-term investors in shares did not pay income tax on capital gains on shares which were bought for long-term gain. There was an arbitrary 12-month rule which taxed gains on shares bought and sold within a year and some investors who made a living from shares paid tax, but generally most people did not have to bother with their capital gains.

At the same time, dividends paid by companies were taxed in the hands of shareholders, after already being taxed in the companies' hands. As this could mean tax at the rate of more than 77 per cent of pre-tax profits flowing to the Federal Government's coffers through company and personal income tax, there was a distinct reluctance on the part of Canberra to alter this system. However, to the credit of the Hawke Government and the then Treasurer, Paul Keating, this was altered from 1 July 1987 to what is generally called a dividend imputation system. Before we look at the system in a little more detail, it is important to realise what this change has meant for Australian companies and investors.

It may seem strange to spend a complete chapter on dividend imputation in a book published six years after the introduction of the new system. In fact, the available evidence suggests that many individual investors are still in the dark about dividend imputation. Stockbrokers and Australian Stock Exchange (ASX) marketing and education people all report that there is very fuzzy knowledge of the advantages of dividend imputation among the general public and potential investors.

When a survey by the ASX in 1988 asked owners of shares — note, not just any members of the public, but people already receiving dividends under the new system — about their knowledge of the new dividend imputation system, more than a quarter of them (25.8 per cent) claimed not to have heard about it. Another 24 per cent had heard about the system but knew very little about it. Only 19 per cent of all share owners could claim to understand a fair amount or a lot about dividend imputation. Three years later, in another ASX survey in 1991, the percentage of shareowners who said they had not heard of dividend imputation had risen slightly from 25.8 per cent to 28.6 per cent. Another 24 per cent still knew very little about it — almost 53 per cent of share owners were basically ignorant of the dividend taxing system. However, in 1988 only 20 per cent of all share owners claimed to understand a lot or a fair amount about dividend imputation but three years later the percentage had risen substantially to almost 34 per cent. Slowly, the 'gospel' about dividend imputation is being preached, mainly by those who stand to benefit most — stockbrokers and financial advisers — and by occasional explanatory articles in the media.

My own experience has been that when a potential investor has the tax advantages of dividend imputation explained to them, their first question is 'But what's the catch?' When you tell them there isn't a catch, except that they have to invest money in shares — perhaps for a number of years — rather than in the bank, they invariably ask for more information. Hence this chapter on dividend imputation. First, though, let's look at what the system is trying to achieve.

THE PURPOSE OF DIVIDEND IMPUTATION

Dividend imputation attempts to reverse the previous bias in the system of company financing which favoured loans rather than share capital. Interest paid on loans can be deducted from pre-tax profits, but under the old system a company paid tax on profits at 39 per cent and then, when the dividends were paid, the shareholders paid tax again on the remaining income. For a major shareholder in a company this effectively was double taxation and financing via loans was more tax-efficient.

The importance of this has not yet become fully apparent, since most listed companies have cut back sharply on new share capital raising in the three years after the 1987 crash, apart from the capital raised by dividend reinvestment plans. But with the traditional lenders, the banks, cutting back or looking more carefully at their lending, equity capital raisings are increasing again.

The main problem in the 1990s will be to find sources of supply of equity funds other than the large institutions which have tended to concentrate on a limited number of major companies. This is where the Federal Government's privatisation program has the opportunity to play an important part in mobilising individual investments into the equity capital market.

The second effect of the twin changes has been to reverse the previous preferences of share investors. In the old days when dividends were taxed and capital gains were not, long-term investors preferred a relatively low dividend payout, with profits ploughed back for expansion. The aim was to achieve strong growth in capital, which was not taxed, rather than rising dividend income, which was taxed.

In addition, shareholders liked a generous use of loan capital to finance expansion to supercharge profits available to them. The over-use of the borrowing strategy — generally called gearing — played a major role in the collapse of most of the high-flying entrepreneurs. We may never be able to distinguish between the legitimate use of borrowings under the pre-1987 dividend system and the over-use by some entrepreneurs who became too hungry for the fruits of geared expansion and the concentration of equity control in their shares. But it is clear that over-borrowing was a major factor in the travails of these companies.

Now, the boards of most companies have realised that it is the total return they can give their shareholders which is important. If in the past they were happy with 25 per cent of their return coming from dividends and 75 per cent from capital gains, now many might be quite happy to see such a ratio reversed. The new strategy for company boards is 'to create wealth for shareholders' and the most tax-efficient way to do that these days is to maximise the benefits from the dividend imputation system.

In general, it has meant that companies concentrate more on increasing dividend payments and less on issuing 'free' shares in what are called bonus issues. Once upon a time, listed company boards believed that they could put potential critics off the scent by leaving the dividend rates unchanged and achieving rises in shareholders' incomes by increasing the number of shares they held. For example, a company could make a one-for-four bonus issue and maintain its dividend at 10 cents a share. Since a holding of 100 shares became 125 shares, dividend income would rise 25 per cent, equivalent to a 12.5 cents a share dividend. Some companies would make regular bonus issues which, even at a modest one-for-ten basis each year, more than doubled the shareholding in eight years — and any dividend rate which was maintained during such a period, of course, also doubled.

HOW THE SYSTEM WORKS

The aim of the dividend imputation system is to treat dividends as income which has already been taxed once (when the company paid tax at the company tax rate of 39 per cent). Provided a company pays dividends from profits on which company tax has been paid, it can declare 'franked' dividends. Depending on the level of company tax paid and the 'franked' dividends paid in earlier periods, a company can declare a dividend to shareholders which is fully franked, partly franked or unfranked. Companies now pay 33 per cent of its pre-tax profit in company tax and the remaining 67 per cent is available to be distributed as a fully franked dividend. Companies have to account for these amounts in a separate franking account because it can hoard the franked credits from year to year if necessary.

A simple example assumes that a shareholder receives a dividend of $100, which is fully franked. The cheque butt or dividend advice from the company will show this:

Amount paid $100.00
Imputation tax credit...$49.25
Amount to be shown as taxable income $149.25

Thus the shareholder is up for tax on $149.25 at the appropriate marginal tax rate; in this example we will assume it is the top rate for 1993–94 of 48.4 per cent (the top rate of 47 per cent plus the Medicare levy of 1.4 per cent).

The tax, however, is offset by that imputation tax credit which is available to be used as a rebate on income tax payable. So the calculation for the shareholder's tax position looks like this:

Tax liability (48.4% of $149.25)........................$72.24
Rebate from franking credit $49.25
Tax payable $22.99

Since we assumed a dividend of $100, we can see at a glance that our taxpayer on the maximum rate of 48.4 per cent actually has paid tax at the rate of only 23 per cent or just under half the maximum tax rate. Some company dividends may still be franked at the earlier 39 per cent tax rate which will give shareholders a lower effective tax rate of 15.4 per cent.

Franking rebates can also be used to 'shelter' other income from salary or wages or from interest on other investments.

Someone earning $2030 a year in income from interest would pay on 1994-95 tax rates $4174 (including Medicare) in taxes. But, assume they could afford to spend about $160,000 to acquire shares yielding about 5 per cent or $8000 of fully franked dividends. The dividends (plus imputation credits) would increase their taxable income to $36,145 (including $5115 of imputation credits created by 39 per cent company tax payments) but would actually decrease their tax payable to $3702.

This is how the sums look:

	Without dividends	With dividends
Interest	$23,030	$23,030
Fully franked dividend		$8,000
Imputation credit		$5,115
Taxable income	$23,030	$36,145
Tax payable (1994-95 rates)	$3,852	$8,311
Medicare (1.4%)	$322	$506
Total tax plus Medicare	$4,174	$8,817
Imputation rebate		$5,115
Amount payable	$4,174	$3,702

The additional $8000 of franked dividend income reduces the total amount payable because the marginal rate applicable to the $36,145 income (34% plus the 1.4% Medicare levy) does not exceed the franking credits available to 'shelter' the tax (that is, the excess imputation credits can be applied to reduce the tax on other income).

Put another way, instead of earning $23,030 from interest and paying tax at an average rate of 18.1 per cent, the taxpayer can mix franked dividends and interest to achieve an average tax rate of about 10.2 per cent

Of course, these calculations depend on franked dividends at least not declining from year to year. However, there is such a growing use of franked dividends by many individual taxpayers that most major company boards are now well aware of the need to maintain the level of franking at a predictable level.

Newcomers to investment should realise there is no suggestion of any tax 'fiddling' in people arranging their income in this way. Would-be investors can approach franked dividends by asking: Given a level of franked dividend income, how much other income can be earned without paying any more tax?

A table from the ANZ McCaughan/Coopers & Lybrand publication, The Australian Dividend Handbook, included in the Appendix, enables this to be calculated in steps of $1000 of fully franked dividends, using 1994-95 tax rates and assuming dividends are franked at 39 per cent.

The Medicare levy cannot be escaped, unfortunately, and this starts to cut in fairly early, though it only exceeds $10 a week once income goes above about $30,000. A mix of dividends and other income can vary from a very low percentage of franked dividends to 100 per cent franked dividends at the top end of the income scale. This means that dividend yields as calculated in the newspapers' tables of share prices understate the return on a pre-tax basis — the basis on which all other investment returns are expressed.

For instance, your savings bank does not offer net interest rates of between 5.175 and 10 per cent (the after-tax returns on a 10 per cent interest rate for taxpayers on the maximum marginal rate and those paying no tax). For a very good reason, too — the net returns depend on the level of the investors' total taxable income. So the best thing to do is to convert the dividend yields on shares back to the same basis as other pre-tax returns. To do this for a fully franked dividend, the dividend yield should be divided by 0.61 or, if multiplication is easier, multiply the yield by 1.64.

As an example, in April 1993 National Australia Bank shares were selling at a dividend yield of 4.32 per cent while savers could have achieved a similar interest rate of, say, 4.2 per cent on some accounts. But our adjustment of the National's share yield back to a pre-tax basis means the shares are offering the equivalent of 6.4 per cent compared with the 4.2 per cent on a bank deposit.

In other words, the National's shares were offering a return of about 50 per cent more than one of their deposits. There was, of course, the usual risk with a dividend that it might not be maintained but it is doubtful if the risk is enough to justify such a differential in pre-tax returns.

In March 1993, the average dividend yield on industrial shares was down to 3.5 per cent or an adjusted 5.2 per cent on a pre-tax basis, well above the best current yield from a cash management trust of 3.8 per cent. The fall in fixed interest yields from 1991 onwards certainly appears to have caused many private investors to move further into shares offering part or full tax-free dividends.

The managing director of leading stockbroker J.B. Were,

Mr Terry Campbell, has a theory that this relationship between share yields and cash management trust returns can be used to determine when private investors should (and do) prefer shares to fixed interest investments. The relationship is certainly one which ordinary investors should consider. Of course, investment decisions need to be based on factors other than pure net returns. But when investors are seeking the best long-term alternative and are not concerned about using the funds in the short term, this yield comparison is worth considering.

The impact of franked dividends is virtually the same whether an individual shareholder receives the dividends or whether the dividend is paid to a local company which can take the franked dividends, add them to any of its own franking credits, and pay its own franked dividends.

Franked credits also are important to superannuation funds which are now taxed at a flat 15 per cent rate on both investment income and on contributions received from members. The super funds can use the franking rebates to reduce the 15 per cent tax. This virtually underwrites support for the share market from most superannuation funds which need to maintain a reasonable level of their funds in shares to minimise their tax.

The advantages of franked dividends also flow through trusts and partnerships and the only investors who do not benefit are overseas shareholders who are subject to a withholding tax which generally cancels out the benefits of the franking credits.

This very superficial look at dividend imputation has been aimed mainly at the implications for the individual investor, who has the greatest potential to benefit from the rebates offered by franked dividends. But one disclaimer: I am not a taxation expert and anyone who intends to take advantage of dividend imputation in income planning should obtain advice from a taxation expert.

9

THE LONG-TERM YIELD

To turn $100 into $110 is work. To turn $100 million into $110 million is inevitable.

— *Edgar Bronfman, chairman of Seagram Co, 1985*

*L*et's review *The Art of Investment* so far. We've discovered:

REVIEW
- Firstly, that returns from bonds just manage to keep pace with inflation, but that shares and property provide much greater returns, with shares returning roughly double the return of bonds and a consistent 'real' return over the long term.
- Secondly, that the greater risk in shares can be controlled by a mixed or diversified portfolio and/or by investing over a time period longer than five or ten years.
- Thirdly, that, apart from the basic trade-off between risk and return, investors need to look to the safety of their investment; to discipline themselves to concentrate on value, flexibility and the right timing; to research their investments; to ensure they have liquidity; and to avoid the extremes of fear and greed in the markets.
- Finally, that the introduction of franked dividends on ordinary shares has given ordinary investors a powerful tax incentive and a tool to increase their actual, net investment returns.

In essence, the pressing need to beat inflation, the long-term record of equity investments and the tax advantages all add up to a simple bottom line: people should be under-taking long-term investment plans using shares.

It is worth defining one thing at this stage: by long-term, I mean a period of about ten years. This definition is per-haps necessary because, even though the excessive concen-tration on short-term returns has been largely wrung out of investors since 1987, there is still some doubt on what constitutes 'long-term' investment. A survey for Roth-schild Australia late in 1990, for instance, revealed that ten per cent of people regarded 'long-term' as from one to three years and that another 21 per cent of people though it involved a five-year period. Just over half of the people surveyed nominated a six- to ten-year period as their idea of 'long-term' suggesting that people are slowly returning to realistic views of investment terms.

WHAT IS
'LONG-TERM'?

For most people, the main choice at this point is whether they want to pay someone else to invest their money or whether they want to manage their own investments. This choice will usually depend on whether our potential investor has the inclination to take what appears to be a gamble on do-it-yourself investment. The nervous or uncertain investor — often encouraged by the sales pitches of salesmen for managed products — will be tempted to take what looks like the safe option and let the experts take over.

MANAGEMENT vs
SELF-
MANAGEMENT

If this decision is really based on an inability to handle investment or a disinclination to gamble with savings, then I have no argument with a choice of a managed investment product. There are many good managers with good track records and reasonable charges. But, again, I should point out that investors in some managed products are paying a very high price for what they think is their ignorance and, in some cases, are getting poor returns.

In the meantime, investors who want to try their hand directly in the share market have a variety of alternatives which are not too expensive and which need not expose them to undue risks.

They could, I suggested in the first edition of this book written in March 1991, buy a parcel of BHP shares. Then, a parcel of 100 BHP cost around $1100, plus $70 to $120, depending on the level of charges levied by a stockbroker. In a little over a year, the parcel of shares would have risen in value to about $1400 while three years after the purchase, the parcel was worth $1650.

During the two years after purchase, BHP paid $40.50 in fully franked dividends on the holding. The franking credits on the dividends amounted to $25.89, producing $66.39 of taxable income. On the then maximum rate of 48.25 per cent (paid by those earning more than $50,000), this resulted in a $32.03 tax bill, reduced by the franking credits to just $6.14 for a net income after tax of $34.36.

Then, in the 1993–94 year, BHP increased the dividend payout to $44. With a $28.13 franking credit, taxable income was $72.13, creating $34.91 of tax at the 48.4 per cent tax rate. The franking credits reduced that tax bill to $9.09, producing a net after tax income of $34.91.

Thus, in the first two years after purchase, BHP was returning around 3.1 per cent after tax on the original purchase price, rising to approaching 3.2 per cent on the original value after the 1993–94 increase in dividend. With lower interest rates producing average cash management trust yields of only about 3.8 per cent in April 1994, investors would be receiving a mere 1.96 per cent after paying the top marginal tax rate on this income. In other words, investors would be more than one and a half times better off after tax in BHP than in a cash management trust — and they would have enjoyed about a 50 per cent capital gain in BHP shares in three years.

Why BHP? For the same reason that many American investors and funds managers buy IBM shares or IBM computers; there is a saying that no-one has ever been sacked for buying IBM. There is a similar attitude in Australia to BHP; it is the largest company on the stock exchange list by such a margin that it is an obvious example to choose. Its past growth record may not be as good as some other fast performers, but it does have one of the longest dividend records and a proud boast that it has not cut a dividend payout for 39 years and not missed a dividend since 1932.

We could just as easily have nominated one of the two long-established investment trusts on the stock exchange list, Argo Investments or Australian Foundation Investment Co (AFIC). Both these stocks invest only in listed industrial shares and pay out most of their profits as fully franked dividends. They have long records of sustained returns, usually at rates above the growth in the share market as a whole. For instance, in the five years to December 1993, when the share market returned an average of 13 per cent a year, Argo's share price rose an average of 12.12 per cent and AFIC's shares rose an average of 18.03 per cent a year. More importantly, as we will see in the next chapter, both companies have achieved annual rates of growth in dividends substantially above the average — Argo's growth in dividends paid in the ten years to 1993 averaged 16 per cent a year and AFIC's growth in dividends was 16.09 per cent a year in the same period.

For small investors, these listed trusts have the additional advantage that the entry costs for the shares are only about one-third those of an unlisted trust and there are virtually no ongoing annual costs.

In addition, the listed investment trusts offer dividend reinvestment plans which allow investors to reinvest their dividends in the same way as unlisted trusts. Above all, the price of the trusts is available on a daily basis and the holdings can be sold and settlement received as soon as share certificates are delivered to the stockbroker.

For a time, these listed investment trusts became so popular that, rather than sell at a discount to their latest net asset backing per share, both Argo and AFIC shares by early 1991 were regularly trading at a premium of up to ten per cent above their asset backing. (The net asset backing is the value of the share portfolio which backs each issued share.) This continued until the second quarter of 1992, before the market price eased back consistently below the net asset backing.

Incidentally, investors seeking 'value' should eschew such situations where they effectively are paying $1.10 to $1.20 for each $1 of shares in the listed investor's portfolio.

Perhaps this seems an over-emphasis on listed investment companies or trusts, but their long-term performance contrasts so much with some of the more recent, unlisted investment trusts that potential investors need to realise the gap in performance and cost of purchase.

AN EXAMPLE OF MANAGED INVESTMENT PERFORMANCE

We can get performance figures for three-year periods covering every type of managed investment product from the ASSIRT research group. Its figures are published every fortnight in the investment paper, *Money Management*. This shows the performance of a selection of managed investment products over a three-year period to March 1993. For comparison, the table includes the performance of appropriate indices which provide benchmarks for the investment managers:

Average return % p.a.

Share trusts:

61 growth trusts	21.8
40 balanced trusts	14.9
All ords accumulation index	19.1

Personal superannuation products:

147 managed growth funds	11.9
38 managed stable funds	7.7
All ords accumulation index	19.1
Wholesale super pooled funds	
— capital stable	13.4
— balanced funds	16.6

Insurance bonds:

91 managed growth bonds	9.0
21 managed stable bonds	6.2
All ords accumulation index	19.1

Property trusts:

29 unlisted growth trusts	−11.8
14 unlisted balanced trusts	−10.0
ASC Prop trusts accum index	+10.8

Fixed interest trusts:

21 mortgage trusts	8.9
21 fixed interest trusts	10.8
Commonwealth Bank bond index	14.2
20 cash management trusts	6.0
SBC bank bills index	7.1

Source: ASSIRT/Money Management

For investors seeking a manager to look after their investments in the share market or to run a diversified fund, those average returns provide food for thought.

In the share market, on average, the balanced fund returns were some 22 per cent below the market return.

And, while the growth trusts on average outperformed the index, this was achieved largely because a third of the 30 outperformers were equity trusts specialising in gold or resources shares which are higher-risk investments.

In the case of superannuation managed products, the returns on average in the retail funds were only about 60 per cent of the average returns acheived in the comparable wholesale fund catefories run by the major investment managers.

And what of those investors who invested in insurance bonds (after all, 'bond' has the connotation of safety, doesn't it?) The results of the insurance bonds were even worse than those of personal superannaution products.

In fact, investors prepared to undertake some simple asset allocation — say one-third in shares, one-third in listed property trusts and one-third in cash management trusts — could have on average outperformed the insurance bond managers with a return of just over 10 per cent.

This poor performance, incidentally, is not necessarily an argument against paying managers to invest your funds; some investment experts do manage to add value to investment portfolios over time. But the poor average returns in many managed investment products at the retail level is more an indication of the high level of charges and commissions which retard the net performance figures.

The performance by managers was much better in the fixed interest area where fixed interest and cash management trusts almost matched the overall performance of bonds and bank bills (with the difference in returns probably accounted for by operating costs, etc.). Similarly, the comparisons of property investments shows that, after an earlier period of apparent outperformance by the unlisted property growth trusts, the recent three-year returns from these former glamour investments have been negative for several years. The larger listed property trusts which, on the same three-year performances in 1990 appeared to be lagging, have edged back into leadership over unlisted trusts.

In summary, many investors in unlisted managed investments have been paying initial charges of perhaps six per cent, plus ongoing fees of perhaps two per cent, for below-average returns.

In the vast array of investment managers offering equity or part-equity, based on three-year performances, there is still only a 50/50 chance of an investor selecting an equity-based product which has done better than the share market index. (Though, to be fair, this is about what you would expect statistically.)

If investors manage to select equity-based products successfully and the managers continue to perform consistently, investors should at least match the averages. But there is an element of doubt and, unless investors select their managed product very carefully, there is a better than average chance of not even matching the averages.

The smart money, however, has identified the best-performing equity trusts. Of the 10 largest trusts, four have achieved returns ahead of the All Ordinaries accumulation index over the last three years. And the strong outperformers have increased their funds under management by three to three and a half times in the space of three years.

THE LARGEST BALANCED SHARE TRUSTS

Manager/Trust	Funds $mill	Rank	Return* % p.a.	Rank
BT Select Growth	1546	1	25.8	2
Perpetual Industrial	839	2	20.5	4
Rothschild	505	3	14.7	7
Advance Imputation	360	4	14.7	6
Westpac Imputation	313	5	13.9	9
Potter Warburg Imputation	272	6	21.6	3
MLC Prop Secs	221	7	11.6	9
MLC index fund	143	8	15.2	5
First State Imputation	130	9	29.5	1
IPAC Aust Equity	80	10	n.a.	n.a.

* Three years to March 1994
Source: ASSIRT/Money Management

As a benchmark, the all ordinaries accumulation index produced a return of 21.9 per cent a year in the same three years. Against that, the best three-year return was from First State's Imputation Fund which returned 15.7 per cent a year. The two biggest trusts — BT Select Growth and Perpetual's Industrial Share Trust — produced returns respectively of 7.4 and 8.6 per cent over the three years. Could an average investor do better than that? The answer is almost certainly 'yes'.

Rather than rely on returns produced by buying a basket of hundreds of stocks in the index, let's look at the results from one private investor's portfolio. In four stocks held for almost 25 years, the capital growth alone in each of the four stocks matched or outstripped those 8–8.5 per cent returns.

EXAMPLE PERFORMANCE OF A PRIVATE INVESTOR'S PORTFOLIO

The growth rates achieved in the stocks were:

Stock	Original cost	Current value	Growth % p.a.
BHP	$591	$12,709	13.0
Boral	$491	$8,563	7.0
Coles Myer	$366	$3,154	9.0
CRA	$3,469	$28,334	8.8

It should be emphasised that these figures show only the growth in the original capital; the subsequent dividends paid would have repaid the original investment many times over, even allowing for the effect of inflation. But, to be conservative, let's merely add the current dividend yields to the growth rates, which suggests BHP could have returned about 16.7 per cent, Boral about 14 per cent, Coles 13.3 per cent and CRA 14.7 per cent. If those returns look too high, remember back to Chapter 1 and the average returns achieved over 25-year periods of around 14 per cent p.a. compound.

What these returns tell us is that an average investor who did hold these four stocks since 1966 would have achieved likely returns of around 15 per cent a year compound. (The BHP and CRA holdings comprised the larger of the four holdings.) There is no fiddling, by picking four of the better performers and then going back to 1966 with perfect hindsight. These stocks were selected by the investor and a stockbroker and held through thick and thin. Only the CRA holding was touched, in two isolated small sales to raise funds. In the other cases, the only action has been to bank the dividends twice a year, every year, without fail.

This investor's portfolio also provides evidence of the large and sustained growth in income from dividends over a long period. Too often, investment books emphasise growth in the capital value of shares, forgetting what has been, in the last decade, outstanding growth in income from dividends.

In the case of Boral, the 1990–91 yearly dividend represented a yield of more than 120 per cent on the original 1966 investment, while the BHP yield was around 70 per cent, CRA's latest dividends represented more than 50 per cent and Coles Myer's 1990–91 dividend represented a yield of almost 40 per cent on the original cost of the shares.

Remember, we are talking about four shares which in early 1994 were yielding between 2.6 per cent and 5.4 per cent from their last annual dividends. As well, the investor did not choose to enrol in the dividend or bonus share reinvestment plans operated by these companies which would have added significantly to the total returns.

LOOKING PAST THE CURRENT YIELDS

As the records over 25 years show, the immediate yield on a share is really only the basement and subsequent growth in the number of shares or in the dividend rate will super-charge dividend yields over a longer period of time.

This was brought home to me when, during a talk I gave in 1990 at the Australian Stock Exchange in Brisbane, an investor asked during question time why potential investors get so worried about a yield of 3.5 per cent on BHP shares? He then explained that he had held BHP shares for some years and with dividends reinvested and bonus shares acquired he knew his yield from his original investment was several times the level of the current yield. It was one of those moments of discovery — for others in the audience as well as for me — since most people think only of the current yields. As I recall saying to the questioner, he had put his finger on a real truth about share investment which non-investors might never discover.

In examples presented by Perpetual Trustee's director of marketing, Peter Thornhill, ten years after investing $1000 in Boral shares, in 1990–91 the last 12 months of dividends would have produced $431 (a handy 43 per cent yield on the original investment), while similar figures for Pacific

Dunlop showed a dividend, ten years after investing $1000, of $340 or 34 per cent on the original amount invested.

In essence, only the initiated investors discover that growth in the capital value of their shares is but one part of the equation. In recent years, dividends paid to investors have risen as much as or more than share prices and have been the main element in investors' gains.

10

TIMING IN THE MARKET

It will fluctuate.

— *J Pierpont Morgan's considered opinion on the stock market*

Despite all the statistics earlier in this book about the medium- and long-term record of capital growth in the share market, it is an unfortunate fact that many people have tried investing in the stock market and have lost money. It is said by cynics around the stock market that there has to be at least ten years between really wild booms, simply to allow for a new generation of gullible speculators, with no burnt fingers from previous booms, to emerge.

The main reason for losses in the stock market is that many people are attracted to the stock market only during a boom, usually very near the top of the boom. The first-time investor comes rushing into the market, eyes alight at the prospect of returns of 30, 40 or 50 per cent a year, asking, 'How long has this marvellous game been going on?' What they don't realise in their excitement is that, at this stage, the stock market is playing a serious game of Pass the Parcel or Musical Chairs and that the newcomers are the innocent cannon fodder for the professionals.

In short, most people who lose money in the stock market lose it because they buy the wrong shares — usually speculative issues such as mining explorers — or because they buy at the wrong time. Even the best leading shares can produce losses for the unwary investor if the share is bought at the peak of a cycle or if it is held for too long.

As one fund manager puts it, the ordinary investor can either overpay or overstay. To avoid doing this, they need to know how to judge when the stock market as a whole is too low or too high and when an individual share is underpriced or overpriced.

As we noted earlier, investors need to distinguish between price and value. Share prices and the level of the share price index are not enough to make a value judgment.

Instead, investors need, in the case of individual shares, to study things like dividend yields, interest rates, earnings per share, price/earnings ratios, the type of company and its position in its market, its financial position and, above all, its management record and skills.

When it comes to the value of the market as a whole, some of these factors also need to be considered, along with the level of economic activity, the supply of money, the level of inflation, and the performance of other stock markets.

THEORY vs PRACTICE IN PROFESSIONAL MANAGEMENT

According to investment theory (as preached by the professional investment managers), the most important thing in achieving good returns is the timing and the allocation of assets in the total investment portfolio. This relates specifically to the professional fund managers who may distribute money in large funds (typically, a superannuation fund) between bonds and cash, shares, property, and overseas shares and bonds.

In theory, an investment manager can outperform others by picking the right time to sell shares before the market falls. Then, after putting the money into cash deposits, he can wait until the stock market reaches bottom before buying shares again. That's the theory, but a cautious manager may sell too early in a really strong boom like 1985–87 and miss a significant part of the rise in the stock market. And, if he leaves funds in cash too long, he also may miss the rebound of the stock market from its low point.

In practice, few of the professional managers handling large portfolios attempt to switch completely out of one asset or into another, because of the risk of mistiming and the costs of selling and buying. They tend to hedge their positions in the stock market by using what are called synthetic investments — options and futures. That is why most investment managers were still holding large positions in the stock market on 21 October 1987, and why they have continued to hold significant levels of shares since then.

More importantly, the managers of large portfolios run by life offices and investment management groups are offering a consistent, long-term product which must be available day after day. This applies both to those portfolios which offer wholesale products (for individual superannuation funds) or retail products (for individual investors). So, in a sense, most professional managers are locked into the stock market or the bond market or the real estate market. They can reduce or increase the percentage holdings (within limits) or they can delay buying or selling until what they judge to be the best time. But, except for a few managers who run specialist funds for clients who know what they want, investment managers cannot realistically quit the stock market if they think it is too high or put most of their funds into cash on short-term deposit.

FLEXIBILITY OF SMALLER INVESTORS

Smaller investors, however, have a distinct advantage over professional investment managers. Small investors can afford to switch around their investments. If they think the stock market is becoming overvalued, they can gradually sell off their holdings. They may apply a stringent test of value, rejecting shares which do not meet their criteria. If they apply these tests rigidly, it may result in them selling many shares and not buying new ones, so that their portfolio purges itself of shares as the stock market becomes overvalued.

There is nothing wrong with this approach, especially in avoiding temptation in a bull market. However, in all but small portfolios, fairly frequent switching can become costly and investors need to weigh the capital protected against the costs and commissions paid. The one exception to this was in October 1987 when the stock market fell by about 25 per cent in one day and, for some stocks, there was never again the same opportunity to sell at boom prices. October 1987 was really the ultimate lesson for those who had become excessively greedy: those who were left had lingered one day too long in the boom market and were given no chance to avoid punishment. By late 1987, there were only two categories of investors: those who had held on for the last profit from the market and those who had anticipated the slump and sold. Never was there a better illustration of the old adage that those who make money in the stock market always sell too early.

Incidentally, newcomers to the market who were not involved in October 1987 need to know what really happened. The folklore is that an entirely unexpected sell-off, triggered by the Wall Street stock market in the US, sent the Australian stock market into its slump. The fact is that the slump was certainly sudden, coming on top of the retreat which had already occurred, but it was by no means unexpected. Informed investors could have avoided the worst effects of the collapse.

Just to see for myself, I went back to the share list for Friday, 16 October, the last trading day before the New York and then the Australian stock markets went over the cliff. The fact is that the day before the collapse many leading stocks had already fallen about ten per cent from their 1987 peak prices and some of the entrepreneurial stocks has already fallen between 20 and 40 per cent from their 1987 peak levels. These were clear warning signs of the carnage still to come and only the greedy ignored the warnings.

If investors adopt the long-term approach to investment — which, from experience, I believe guarantees success — by the time the stock market becomes overvalued, they may not need to worry about protecting their position.

For instance, that private investor whose holdings were used as an example in Chapter 9 has owned CRA shares for almost 30 years and holds the shares at an average cost of about $1.50. Even if CRA shares looked overvalued at prices of $11 or $12, there is no danger of a fall in the shares inflicting actual losses to the cost price. The only reason to sell a stock in this situation would be if the share looked overvalued *and* the stock comprised a disproportionately large part of the share portfolio.

'DOLLAR AVERAGING' TO COVER MARKET SWINGS

Small investors are at a disadvantage in that they have to make proportionally larger bets than the big managers. A small investor may have to commit 50 or even 100 per cent of the available funds to investment at one time. The large institution has a regular inflow of funds to invest, each purchase representing a much smaller percentage of the total portfolio and the big players can average out purchases over the ups and downs of markets.

Small investors can do this by using the 'dollar averaging method'. This involves investing an equal amount of money at regular intervals, often monthly. The reason to adopt this approach is simple. No one knows what the market will do next. Even one of the legendary speculators, J Pierpont Morgan, when asked what the market would do, could give no more precise a forecast than the legendary reply: 'It will fluctuate.'

Example: An investor invests $1000 each quarter in a share where the price is, in successive quarters: $10, $5, $4 and $10. At the end of a year, the investor has spent $4000 and has 650 shares bought at an average price of $6.15 each.

This is fine in theory, but in Australia it probably requires investors to commit large amounts to the exercise. The reason: The minimum brokerage charges on four $1000 transactions could add up to charges equal to ten per cent in four orders. Unless an investor has an understanding broker, dollar averaging is perhaps best handled by regular investment plans run by some managed investment group.

Small investors have another averaging on their investments — using dividend reinvestment plans. Most major companies operate these plans which enable investors to be paid in shares rather than receive cash dividends. Most of the plans offer the shares at discounts of between five and ten per cent off the average market price and the purchases are free of brokerage or stamp duty. At least one major company, CSR Ltd, also offers a share purchase system where shareholders can contribute up to $2400 a year to buy new shares at a discount.

Excluding the use of these averaging techniques, the small investor in the stock market has two challenges: to pick the right time to buy and sell and to pick the right stocks. Perhaps describing that merely as a challenge is as much an understatement as the statement by a wife who said she only disliked two things about her husband: everything he said and everything he did.

Let's concentrate first on the question of the right time. The main argument so far in *The Art of Investment* has been that investing in shares over the long term guarantees capital gains. But not everyone may have the patience to wait for 10 or 20 years to be proved comprehensively correct. It is clear that improving the timing can produce much better results.

PICKING THE RIGHT TIME

For example, someone who bought into the stock market in June 1968 would have run into three losing years, one year of sharp recovery and then another three years of losses. The average growth rate for shares held over the ten years to June 1978 would have been only 2.8 per cent a year. Even so, if that investor had persisted with the holdings, over a 21-year period to the end of 1989, the annual return would have recovered to 11.5 per cent compound (or a growth of $100 to $1000).

But even if the passage of time eventually will soothe some of the short-term losses from bad timing, no-one wants to invest and then face immediate capital losses, so the question is: what do investors watch for as a signal that the share market is underpriced or overpriced?

Well, in our example of someone who bought in June 1968, there was a fairly easy way of avoiding that mistake — by looking at the immediate past. The stock market as measured by the all ordinaries index had risen more than 74 per cent in the previous 12 months. It was, of course, the Poseidon nickel boom and fundamental values were lost in a rush of speculation which spread to industrial shares from the booming mining market.

A rise of less than half that rate should have been enough to trigger the warning bells; the 1960 and 1961 downturns had followed four booming years which saw the market rise at an average annual rate of about 24 per cent compound. As a rough working rule, rises in the stock market at rates of more than double the normal long-term trend of about ten per cent should be treated with suspicion if sustained for several years.

Perhaps this looks too easy. Do we simply watch the old rule that whatever goes up sharply must also come down sharply? Surely there must be a more sophisticated method of timing share purchases. My view is that the simplest tests are often the best, as long as we can keep our heads.

But the nature of speculative booms is that, in every one I can remember, people find it hard to keep their heads. At some stage in every boom you will hear a common cry, 'But this boom is different'.

During the last boom, which lasted essentially for almost five years and much longer than most past booms, people began to believe that the world had somehow found a way to keep share and other asset prices rising indefinitely. It wasn't put as bluntly as that, of course, since too many people would have recognised the fallacy. Instead, we were told that the politicians and authorities had found a way of smoothing out the business cycles, those nasty cycles in the economy which coincide with the ups and downs in the stock market. In fact, all that had happened in Australia and in some other markets was that we had a period of deregulation in the financial system which, along with other factors, produced a high level of money supply which was financing the boom.

So, the first weapon which investors can use to finetune their timing in the stock market is plain old common sense.

WATCH INTEREST RATES

Apart from this first line of defence, many people would nominate interest rates as perhaps the first test of value in the stock market. Indeed, some valuation models produced by stockbroking and institutional analysts often rely on a relationship between share yields and long-term bond yields. I have some doubts about relying too much on a relationship between interest rates and the share market. There is no doubt that there was a close correlation in the 1960s and part of the 1970s when the long-term bond yield and share yields tracked each other fairly closely, but we have now seen more than 15 years when the ten-year bond yield has been persistently above the yield on shares — in some cases of up to seven per cent.

However, the recent falls in the US and local bond markets have reminded share investors there is a strong short-term correlation between interest rates and shares. Even today a major shift up or down in bond and bank bill yields will usually send share prices down or up. There are two reasons: comparative investment yields, and the effect on company profits.

Since investors choose between yields on shares and yields on interest rate securities like cash management trusts, a fall in yields on cash management trusts will improve the attractiveness of share yields. In addition, lower interest bills will enable companies to increase their net profits. The reverse applies in the case of interest rates increasing.

This relationship between comparative yields is one reason for some of the bullishness in the stock market in the early 1990s. In the last three years to 1993, inflation rates were reduced to less than three per cent a year. This saw short-term interest rates come down from about 15 per cent to 5 per cent, but average share yields on industrial shares fell from 6.8 per cent to around 3.5 per cent in the same period.

Remember the adjustment factor for franked dividend yields of about 1.5; this multiplication factor means that dividend yields of 3.5 per cent become competitive with bill rates of 5.25 per cent.

WATCH COMPANY PROFITS

While investors can only hope for a period of sustainable low inflation in Australia, something we have not seen for almost three decades, the fact is that in the last decade and a half company profits and dividends have been the driving force in the stock market. Since the 1975 recovery in the stock market, company profits (and earnings per share) have been largely propelling share prices, except for the period in the last years of the 1980s boom when take-over activity and paper shuffling drove many share prices until the general speculation which ran out in October 1987. Now, the market tends to depend on the forecasts of earnings by analysts and there has been a very close relationship between company earnings and the stock market in a period between 1975 and 1982, as shown in the Armstrong Jones graph over page.

The relationship between prices and earnings is expressed in the stock market by the price/earnings ratio,

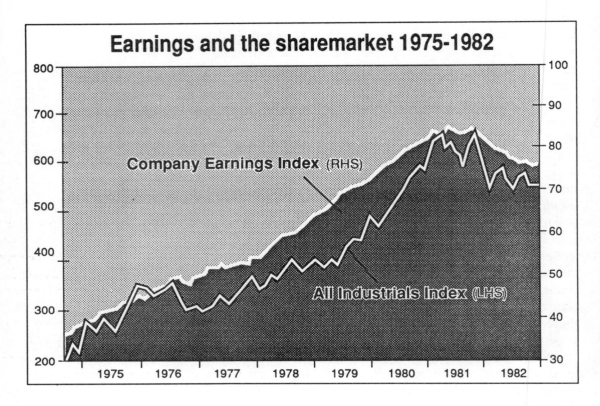

Earnings and the sharemarket 1975-1982

Company Earnings Index (RHS)

All Industrials Index (LHS)

often shortened to P/E ratio or alternatively called the earnings multiple. It is calculated by dividing the earnings per share (in cents) into the share price. The use of the P/E ratio can be extended to a measure of the market as a whole or for a particular sector such as the all industrials index.

The P/E ratios published in the newspaper share market tables relate to historical earnings, so the ratios are most accurate from July to December when the earnings for the financial year to June 30 become available to the market. Clearly, by July the year after a profit has been reported, the P/E ratio will be based on information more than 12 months old. As a result, many analysts now use their estimates of prospective profits for their P/E ratios and talk in terms of a share selling on a prospective P/E ratio.

This fuzziness in P/E ratios means that the average investor needs to use them with some care since the readily available figures can be misleading. For instance, where the

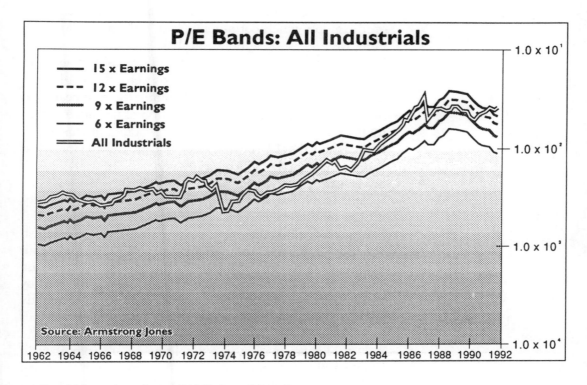

P/E Bands: All Industrials

- 15 x Earnings
- 12 x Earnings
- 9 x Earnings
- 6 x Earnings
- All Industrials

1.0 x 10¹
1.0 x 10²
1.0 x 10³
1.0 x 10⁴

Source: Armstrong Jones

1962 1964 1966 1968 1970 1972 1974 1976 1978 1980 1982 1984 1986 1988 1990 1992

market believes profits will fall sharply in the current year, the share price will drop, sending the P/E ratio to a low level. In this case, the general rule that a low P/E ratio is a good thing would be positively misleading for investors and such misleading P/E ratios can also distort the P/E ratio of the whole market.

There are, however, useful approaches which can be used with P/E ratios. One is to study the range of ratios which apply over a long period to individual shares or to the market as a whole. This can be expressed either by quoting the normal range of earnings multiples which have applied in the past or by expressing the current P/E ratio in terms of the historical average for the stock.

For the market as a whole, an adaptation of this approach can produce a reasonably meaningful measure of over- or under-priced shares.

The graph on the previous page shows how the industrial share market has sold at gradually rising P/E ratios over the last 30 years.

More to the point, by drawing an upper and lower 'band' on the graph which corresponds to a 'high' and a 'low' P/E ratio, we can see how industrial share prices have behaved. For instance, in two cases in the mid-1960s and again in the 1970s, when industrial P/E ratios went above 14 times the index subsequently declined. Similarly, it appeared to bounce off the lower band of a P/E ratio of 6 times earnings in 1975 and launch itself into the 1980s from that level. It breached the 14 times upper band in the madness just before the October 1987 crash and the 14 times upper level again provided resistance in 1988.

This graph suggests a few rules of thumb on P/E ratios for the market as a whole. A level of 14 times or more is a danger signal for the market; a level of 6 times is a bullish sign for the market. In analysing the P/E ratios for the all industrials or the all ordinaries indices, investors should use the figures in the index-linked series of figures released by the ASX rather than the unadjusted ones which generally show a much higher P/E ratio. The other, fairly obvious message from the 1980s is that when the P/E ratio of the industrial share market as a whole has risen from about 6 times earnings to more than 18 times earnings in the space of five years, the stock market is in a bullish and overpriced phase.

One final illustration to emphasise that time, rather than timing, is what ultimately matters in share investment is provided by a booklet from Macquarie Investment Management called *Growth Investments can help secure your future*. A theoretical exercise assumed $5000 was invested in the share market each financial year between 1 July 1980 and 30 June 1993. The exercise looked at the returns from investing the $5000 each year at the best time (the year's low point on the index), the worst time (at the index yearly high) and at a predetermined day of 1 July.

Over the 13 years, investing the total of $65,000 on the worst possible day still produced a final figure of $142,613 for an average return of 11.73 per cent a year. Investing on the best possible day produced a final $199,423 result, while a regular 1 July investment each year showed growth to $179,840, for an average return of 13.92 per cent (The calculations assumed dividends were reinvested.)

In other words, while there was a noticeable difference

between the best and the worst times, picking the best point each year only improved the dollar return by some 11 per cent over the 13 years compared with investing on the same date.

So far we have looked only at the effects of interest rates and company earnings on the stock market. These are what we might call the nuts and bolts of investment, but we need to look at more broader influences as well: notably, economic activity, the money supply inflation and the effects of other markets.

BROADER INFLUENCES ON THE MARKET

Years ago, the stock market was presented as a barometer of the economy, an instrument for measuring the coming moods of the economic weather. Today there is less belief in this aspect of the stock market's powers, although whenever people are looking for signs of economic recovery, they examine the stock market's entrails more closely than usual for the first signs of recovery.

There is a general belief, however, that the progress of the stock market runs roughly parallel with the growth of the economy and that a downturn in activity — as we saw in Australia in 1990–91 — is reflected in the stock market. There is no neat correlation between the two, however, because the stock market is essentially a forward-looking mechanism, whereas we do not get the official 'scores' on the economy until some months after the event. In fact, the stock market rose about 30 per cent in 1991 before the national accounts for the year to December 1991 were released, showing that, at least based on official statistics, the recession had bottomed and that some slight economic growth had resumed.

All the correlations between the stock market and the economy are seen best in very long-term graphs, which is handy for economic history but of little use to investors seeking guidance on the near-term performance of the stock market.

There used to be a saying among the more optimistic economists that the stock market had forecast nine of the last four recessions. Certainly, stock market watchers and economists in the financial markets tend to be very quick on the trigger when it comes to forecasting recessions or recoveries. It has to be said that the 1990–92 recession, when it finally did come, must have been a relief to many economists and forecasters who were warning people from November 1987 of a severe recession or even a depression after the stock market collapse.

The lack of a depression and the fact that a recession was postponed by two years shows that our modern economic managers have learned something over the years, even if they merely postponed the evil day. The 1990–91 recession might not have been, as Paul Keating put it, the recession we had to have, but it was inevitable given the collapse in asset values right around the world which was signalled in October 1987 on the stock markets. Once the Australian Government began to tighten monetary policy (which it had loosened in an immediate policy reaction to the October 1987 slump), it was only a matter of time before the fall in values spread through the economic system to attack real estate, companies holding investments in real assets and, eventually, the banking system.

A more useful indicator is the level of growth in the money supply. When you get right down to it, the stock exchange is purely a market and markets can exist only when buyers have the money to bid for stock. If there is an excess of money supply in the economy — as we saw in the post-1985 period — then the stock market soars as money becomes available for speculative activities, whether straight share buying, speculative corporate activities or company takeovers.

Compared with the middle 1960s when monetarism was all the fashion and the monthly release of money supply figures was given the same attention as, say, the monthly balance of payments figures receive now, few people are interested in money supply. Just the same, investors would do well to monitor money supply figures and a subscription to the *Reserve Bank of Australia Bulletin* is one way of getting regular figures on money supply.

Inflation is another powerful economic factor which, instinctively, investors feel must affect the share market. Inflation, in fact, affects everything in the economy; it is very much like a virus which infects computer programs. Inflation affects people's perceptions about things like prices and rates of returns on investments. It distorts balance sheets and profit and loss accounts, and it can increase tax liabilities.

The major problem with inflation is that it becomes one of the two main targets of economic policy. In very over-simplified terms, economic policy making can be seen, at the two extremes, as either a battle to curb inflation or a battle to prevent unemployment. When unemployment looms, economic policy can be eased (often including interest rates, which is often the easiest policy lever to pull). When inflation threatens to rise, policy can be tight-ened and interest rates are jacked up, as we saw in 1989–90.

Rising interest rates are bad news for the stock market since they usually signal a shortage of money for invest-ment, a fall in bond prices (and rising yields on bonds and shares), higher dividend yields and thus lower share prices and increased costs for companies, reducing net profit and potential dividends.

Relative inflation rates are also a problem for investors, since a higher inflation rate in Australia means that our costs are rising faster than those overseas, such as in the US or Japan, making local companies less competitive. This puts pressure on the Australian currency via rising imports and easing exports so that, to keep attracting over-seas capital into Australia to finance our deficit we have to keep interest rates higher here than they are overseas.

This brings us to the final indicator of relative value in the stock market: what is happening to other world stock markets. We need to keep Australia's place in the world investment markets in perspective; in terms of the total market value of all share markets around the world, Australia's total market value amounts only to about 1.5 to 2 per cent of the world. We are very small beer in world markets and the Australian market leads in really only one respect — after the even smaller New Zealand market, ours is the first market to open each day. Most of the time, the day-to-day sentiment in our market is influenced by what happened the previous night on Wall Street and in London, and by what happens in Tokyo and Hong Kong during our trading day, especially if Asian investors place orders on the Australian market. So the level of the Aus-tralian share market should be measured daily and over a period of time with the major world markets. If our market is moving out of step for a reasonable period, then it is time to look again at the values here. In general, comparing levels of the share market indices is probably the safest international comparisons for the average investor, since it needs a fair amount of detailed knowledge to compare international price/earnings ratios or dividend yields.

The truth of the matter when it comes to timing is perhaps best summed up by two of the more humble, if successful, stock pickers in recent years, Fidelity's Peter Lynch and Templeton International's founder, Sir John Templeton.

Says Lynch: 'Trying to predict the direction of the market over one year, or even two years is impossible.' More colourfully, he advises those who think they can predict market movements that 'If you wake up in the morning and think to yourself "I'm going to buy stocks because I think the market will go up this year," then you ought to pull the phone out of the wall and stay as far away as possible from the nearest broker.' (*One Up on Wall Street*, Simon and Schuster.)

Says Templeton, one of the most successful long-term international investment managers: 'I never ask if the market is going to go up or down next month. I know that there is nobody that can tell me that.' Rather, he researches stocks to find undervalued shares and buys them. As for market timing, he argues the true counter-cyclical view: 'The time of maximum pessimism is the best time to buy and the time of maximum optimism is the best time to sell.' (*Global Investing — The Templeton Way*, Dow Jones Irwin.)

11

COPING WITH A LOW INFLATION ENVIRONMENT

...there is no subtler, no surer means of overturning the existing basis of society than to debauch the currency.

— John Maynard Keynes, 1919

Inflation is a form of financial fraud.

— the Coalition's Fightback! package, 1991

Inflation is a totally corrupting influence on the fabric of society.

— the Federal Government's One Nation statement, 1992

*A*part from the October 1987 collapse and the introduction of dividend imputation, perhaps the greatest change in the Australian investment climate has been the fall in the inflation rate in the early 1990s. Anyone who doubts the degree of change needs only to contemplate those introductory quotations from the policy documents of the two major political parties. Allowing for the usual political rhetoric, both sides of politics now have inflation on their hate list.

The degree of the change needs to be recognised, not only in terms of the local scene, but also in the world context. The annual inflation rate of 1.9 per cent shown by Australia's Consumer Price Index for the year to December 1993 was the lowest annual inflation rate in the 24 western countries which make up the OECD. This is a sharp contrast with the 1970s and 1980s when Australia's inflation rate was persistently among the highest in the OECD economies.

Even more significant than the actual fall in the inflation rate is the change of mood. Expectations about the future level of inflation have also fallen sharply and are continuing to remain low. This has been a major achievement since, in the past, when Australia's inflation rate was reduced briefly there was widespread public belief that the fall was only temporary. Economists argue that the killing of inflationary expectations in the 1990s recession has probably been the major economic achievement.

Unfortunately, the long run of history in Australia suggests that inflation has been running this century at around five per cent a year and that we have only managed to get the rate for the last 10 years down to an average of 5.3 per cent. This has meant that it has taken some time for most investors to change their thinking on inflation. Those investors and investment managers old enough to remember when inflation was last down to two or three per cent are now well into their 50s.

The lesson of history is that sometime in the future inflation will re-emerge as a problem for the investment markets. In the meantime, however, most people are now working on the assumption that low inflation is here for the foreseeable future. While there is still an understandable scepticism based on the history of inflation in Australia, the fact of such a slow economic recovery tends to suggest that inflation could well be slow to re-awaken in Australia.

For long-term investors, this provides a challenge: how to maintain overall returns in the absence of the main driving force behind higher investment returns. The classic government's method of dealing with inflation is to drive up interest rates. While high interest rates are the bane of business life and curb borrowers of capital, they provide higher income levels for investors who have lent their capital.

THE DANGERS   There are two dangers when investors start worrying about how to maintain returns: first that they will be tempted into more risky investments to maintain a nominal rate of return, and second that they will fail to distinguish

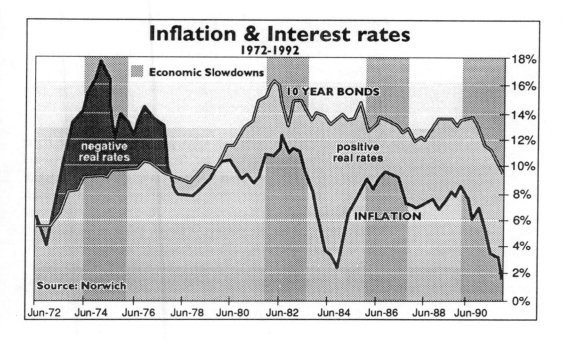

Inflation & Interest rates
1972-1992

Economic Slowdowns

10 YEAR BONDS

negative real rates

positive real rates

INFLATION

Source: Norwich

18%
16%
14%
12%
10%
8%
6%
4%
2%
0%

Jun-72 Jun-74 Jun-76 Jun-78 Jun-80 Jun-82 Jun-84 Jun-86 Jun-88 Jun-90

between nominal and real rates in looking at investment returns.

The graph shows the extent of high real rates of interest, notably at present and at the end of the early 1980s recession. Unlike in the 1970s, when real interest rates were allowed to remain negative and lenders were ripped off, interest rates in subsequent recessions have turned sharply positive in real terms.

But there are still traps, even if people mentally make allowances for real returns, after inflation. The problem is that the after-tax return can shrink alarmingly. Ten year returns calculated by Towers Perrin for the ASX show that a 14.4 per cent average return on bonds was reduced to 7.8 per cent after tax at the maximum rate while a 13.2 per cent p.a. average return on cash management trusts was reduced to only 5.7 per cent by tax — only a fraction above the 10-year inflation rate of 5.3 per cent.

Many investors are still struggling to come to grips with the decline in interest rates as inflation rates have declined. After 1987, many investors put their savings into capital guaranteed funds run by the life offices which were offering interest rates well into double figures. Those returns have now fallen sharply. Many retired people invested for income in 90-day bank bills. In the space of less than two years, returns from bank bills fell from 16–17 per cent to around 6 per cent. For retired people living on investment income, that was the equivalent of having their pension cut by more than 50 per cent — and that's before tax.

Many retired people have paid a high price for their reliance almost exclusively on fixed interest investments as inflation has fallen rapidly. They have made the mistake of not having a diversified investment portfolio which could be readjusted, if necessary, to deal with changed circumstances. This is partly because people have been largely conditioned to think of shares as an investment involving capital growth rather than income, and as inflation has subsided many people have wrongly assumed that there is less place for shares in a portfolio.

Many people are now realising that shares also can produce very good income over the longer term and, as a result, we have seen retired money moving from fixed interest investments back into the share market in search of higher returns. The fact that this has happened and has continued through to the end of 1993 is a sign of the growing recognition of the advantages of investing in shares. Once again, investors will need to be careful that they do not repeat the same mistakes they made in the late 1980s by putting all their eggs in one basket.

Already, the first lesson of investment in a low inflationary environment is fairly clear: diversify your investments.

DIVERSIFY TO SURVIVE

It should be obvious for people investing fixed interest capital that they should diversify, both in where the money is invested and the length of maturity of individual investments. This is the prudent way to minimise the risk of any capital loss and to minimise the risk of having most of your investments locked into the wrong area.

People should always plan or seek expert advice on staggering the maturities of fixed interest investments so that not all their investments mature at the same time. They also, of course, should attempt to stagger the dates on which they receive interest payments to attempt to smooth their income stream.

But the question of diversification goes much deeper than that. A properly diversified portfolio will enable an investor to pick the eyes out of the best-yielding investment opportunities, consistent with their risk profile. A balanced portfolio diversifies investors into shares, bonds, debentures and listed property trusts, all of which have something to offer.

It is also important for people to know what they should avoid during periods of low inflation. The most obvious thing to shun are collectables or tangible assets such as paintings, works of art, antique cars or whatever other assets might have fallen in price. These assets really are worth what people will pay for them rather than what they might earn. And, if there is a sudden shortage of entrepreneurs with easy money to buy Van Goghs or Streetons or antique cars, the prices of these assets will fall whatever their previous values. Remember Rule 3 in Chapter 5 and the difference between value and price.

INVESTMENTS TO AVOID

Unless people have a genuine interest in collecting such assets, they are better off sticking to investments which produce some returns because income is what people really need in times of low inflation when investment returns are depressed. Similarly, a house is fine to own as a place to live, but not necessarily the place to invest money in times of low inflation. The advantages of tax-deductible interest on loans in gearing a real estate investment can, of course, improve the economics of such an investment, but investors need at least to get an alternative opinion before undertaking geared investment. Shares or other securities may well be more appropriate than real estate.

Because of lower investment returns, many people believe low inflation is a bad thing for investors but this is over-simplifying the position. Higher inflation means more uncertainty and more volatility in investment markets. It sends the wrong signals to investors, companies and, collectively, the whole economy.

ADJUSTING TO LOW INFLATION

If Australian policy-makers maintain their stance on inflation and are not scared by high unemployment figures for another year or so, we are clearly going to be facing a future in business and investment which will be very different from the situation 10 or 20 years ago. That is why people should quickly adjust their thinking to the new low inflation environment. It probably means the roaring bull markets which we saw in the 1970s and 1980s are gone for a decade. Investors will not be able to buy anything blindly and then rely on rising market prices to cover up any mistakes.

As American economist and writer John Kenneth Galbraith remarked back in 1970, 'genius is a rising market'. The truth of this was never better illustrated than in the 1980s when easy credit policies enabled speculators to borrow and push up the prices of most assets.

Hopefully, everyone has learned from this, though on past experience the passage of about a decade is all that is needed to allow a new generation of investors to be duped. In the meantime, everyone should make a habit of looking at returns and rates in real terms.

Many people are suggesting that, since we look as though we are returning to levels of inflation last seen here in the early 1960s, we should look back at the interest rates and returns which applied in that period. Unfortunately, so much has changed in the investment world that we could easily mislead ourselves if we slavishly followed the 1960 model.

For a start, Australia is now part of the international investment world and not a small, isolated market. With bond yields, for instance, this means that foreign investors can buy and sell bonds, introducing a lot more opinions on Australia's economic future, its likely inflation rate and the level of our currency. In other investment markets, the fact that we are part of a world market means that interest rates and yields in the largest financial centres of the world affect our markets. Also, we no longer have artificial constraints like the old 30/20 rules forcing institutions to hold minimum levels of government securities. Nor are bank and other interest rates controlled as they were in the 1960s. There are taxes on capital gains and rebates on dividends; in short, a whole new investment game with new rules.

So, investors must face a world where not only are prospective returns looking much lower than in the 1980s but the whole world is a lot more sophisticated and there are no sheltered local markets.

In times of low inflation and lower investment returns, investors really have only three ways to improve their returns: to diversify their portfolio, to seek higher returns, and to minimise taxation on their income.

IMPROVING RETURNS

The sort of returns which investors may need to grapple with over the rest of the 1990s are shown in this table of possible investment returns from Australian investments in the 1990s (compared with actual returns from the 1980s):

Asset	Real returns p.a.	
	1990s	1980s
Shares	7%	8.6%
Fixed interest	5%	3%
Property	3%	7%
Cash	4%	5%

Source: Norwich Investment Management

An additional question raised by the Norwich forecasts (and almost certainly by other forecasts) is whether, in the 1990s, real returns in the major overseas markets could be running much higher than in Australia. For instance, the life office's investment team estimates that German shares could be returning 9 per cent real, that UK fixed interest returns could be higher, and that US and UK property returns could be double that low Australian return of 3 per cent.

Does that suggest individual Australian investors should consider investing some of their funds overseas? It may not be mandatory but it certainly suggests that, in a low return environment, investors can ill-afford to ignore higher returns available overseas.

A fairly conservative allocation of 40 per cent in local shares, 30 per cent in fixed interest, 10 per cent in property, 10 per cent in cash and 10 per cent in overseas shares could produce a return in real terms averaging around 5.8 per cent based on Norwich's estimated returns. A comparable portfolio in the 1980s would have produced about 7 per cent in real returns. What those returns might not show, however, is that returns in the 1990s are likely to be more volatile than in the 1980s and 1970s, so investors deciding on asset allocations might need to weigh carefully their level of exposure to local and overseas shares, since these have traditionally shown the most volatile trend in returns. However, careful asset allocation should be able to help investors match their required returns with the degree of risk they are prepared to accept. The important thing will be for investors to remember that rather than the 1990s returns being lower than the 1980s, it is really the case of abnormal returns from the 1980s settling back to more normal returns in the 1990s.

There undoubtedly will be higher returns available in some areas. The emerging share markets in developing countries are one area where above-average returns should be available. Several skilled investment managers have emerging market equity funds which enable investors to take a modest punt on these high return/high risk markets.

In 1992, the high return areas on the local stock market have been the bank shares, with relatively high dividend yields for blue chip companies, and property trusts, whose dividend yields were nudging double figures. In 1993, the whole share market produced very high returns, averaging 45 per cent based on the All Ordinaries index.

REDUCING TAX

For retired investors, the financial planners will probably be able to find a few other ways of increasing actual returns such as using fixed term cash-back annuities rather than straight fixed interest investments and using cash management accounts or bank 'deeming' accounts rather than ordinary savings accounts.

However, for most investors, the single best way of improving net, real returns is to reduce the tax payable, perhaps also arranging their affairs so that they receive a part pension and take advantage of the pensioner tax concessions.

This might seem like tax fiddling, but reducing tax liabilities is a legitimate target for any investment plan, provided it does not dominate investment thinking and, of course, provided it is within the law.

Obvious ways of reducing the impact of tax on investment returns is to borrow funds to finance part of the investment and claim the interest paid on the loan as a deduction from taxable income —so-called 'gearing'. Or income can be split by putting investments in both partners' names and to maximise tax credits available from fully franked share dividends.

One final point: investors may need to re-think their attitude to what are appropriate dividend yields and price/earnings ratios on shares in a low inflation environment. If a six per cent dividend yield is acceptable at a time of six to seven per cent inflation, surely three per cent or less is similarly suitable at times of three or four per cent inflation — remembering the additional returns from the tax assistance from fully franked dividends.

The Australian Stock Exchange recently has instituted a regular series which shows comparable after tax returns on various investments which demonstrates the superior performance of shares in the last 10 years. Using the maximum marginal tax rate, shares produced a 13.8 per cent a year return against 10.6 per cent from residential property, 7.8 per cent from bonds and only 5.7 per cent from cash management trusts.

THE RULE OF 20

Price/earnings ratios are a little harder to assess, though there is at least one very useful rule of thumb which many investors now use. This is called the Rule of 20 and it simply says that the price/earnings ratio and the rate of inflation should add up to 20.

One investment veteran, James Cowan, says that he first learnt of this rule in 1986 from the senior US investment director of Fidelity International. It applies particularly to markets as a whole and it simply encapsulates the theory that when inflation is high, so are interest rates, which in turn bring down price/earnings ratios. Then, when inflation falls, so do interest rates and price/earnings ratios usually move higher.

James Cowan has produced a table (see overleaf) covering the last 30 years for the Australian stock market which effectively demonstrates the applicability of the rule. In the three decades for which he has calculated the Rule of 20, the average level has come out at almost 20 (in precise terms, 19.97).

In 1992 and the boom 1993 year, the measure has risen to 24, but after the February–March correction in 1994, the measure is back to about 18 in mid-1994.

AUSTRALIAN STOCK MARKETS AND THE RULE OF 20

Year	P/E Ratio	CPI (% p.a.)	Total
1971	10.9	6.1	17.0
1972	16.1	5.9	22.0
1973	10.0	9.5	19.5
1974	6.4	15.1	21.5
1975	8.8	15.1	23.9
1976	7.3	13.5	20.8
1977	7.3	12.3	19.6
1978	6.5	7.9	14.4
1979	7.5	19.1	26.6
1980	10.7	10.1	20.8
1981	11.1	9.7	20.8
1982	9.6	11.1	20.7
1983	12.1	10.1	22.2
1984	11.2	4.0	15.2
1985	14.1	6.7	20.8
1986	15.9	9.1	25.0
1987	12.7	8.5	21.2
1988	14.4	7.2	21.6
1989	13.3	7.6	20.9
1990	11.0	7.3	18.3
1991	15.6	1.5	17.1
1992	21.2	1.2	24.0
1993	22.1	1.9	24.0

More interestingly, in terms of the present period of low inflation, it shows that levels of around 17 to 18 times are virtually in line with levels in the first few years of the 1960s. In 1961 when inflation was 2.5 per cent, price/earnings ratios were 16.1 times on average, rising slightly to averages of 17 and 16.6 times in the next two years when inflation was negative at −1.5 per cent.

The 1992 measure continued the trend of 1990 and 1991 when James Cowan calculated the 30 September measures at 18.3 and 17.1 times respectively. Interestingly, the Rule of 20 gave danger signals in September 1972, just before a period when the stock market lost almost 25 per cent of its value. Similarly, in 1986 and 1987 the rule was screaming 'sell' with measures of 25 and 29.4 respectively.

James Cowan also believes the Rule of 20 can provide useful timing signals of when to buy, taking as an example a time when the Rule of 20 number is 17.5 or less. Buying in these years has, over the last 30 years, produced an average gain in the next year averaging close to 20 per cent.

What the Rule of 20 shows is that provided investors spend some time applying a simple rule to the levels of inflation and the valuation of the stock market, they can assess the level of risk in the market as a whole or the potential opportunities for buying.

A final point for share investors in low inflationary times: the markets will probably pay a premium for shares in companies with higher than average growth potential. This suggests that investors may have to range beyond the small group of market leaders to discover some more growth-prone stocks. This also may mean that the range of acceptable valuations (or price/earnings ratios) may become wider and that investors will have to accept more volatile returns in some stocks. Whether this is worth accepting to achieve higher returns clearly is a matter of choice by individual investors.

Many companies will continue to reduce their gearing levels since, in times of low inflation, there is less to be gained by carrying high levels of borrowings. This will probably put more pressure on the market to supply new share capital, in addition to the likely demands for capital to privatise some government enterprises or to re-capitalise some unlisted groups. This suggests that companies with smaller capitals or tightly held share capital may go to a premium on the market.

In general, then, there appear to be enough positives for the share market to allow small investors to continue to use shares to achieve higher returns, both in actual returns and in better returns on an after-tax basis. But it will be a time when investors will also need to be prudent and not invest all their savings in one basket or one asset class.

12

MORE ON PICKING STOCKS

Success is more a function of consistent common sense than it is of genius.

— An Wang, *founder of Wang Laboratories*

Ask an investment expert how to pick a stock and you will receive a bewildering variety of tips. The problem is that some renowned 'stock pickers' operate partly on instinct and partly on the accumulated knowledge, skill and cunning acquired over many years of operating in the business. Asking them how to pick stocks is like asking a crack shot to explain how he hits moving targets.

At the other extreme, many investment experts pick stocks by using a variety of mechanical methods, which may range from the use of fairly simple criteria to very complicated filter tests run by computer systems.

THEORIES ABOUT SELECTION Some people have theories in selecting stocks, just as punters have sure-fire ways of selecting which horses to back. The trouble is that the success or otherwise of many methods lies more in the mind of the user than in any objective results.

One theory is to select stocks with a recent record of rapidly increasing earnings because this will attract growth and enable rising dividends. If investors want to use this approach, the Australian Stock Exchange (ASX) Statex Research Studies produces a return called *Investor Return and Growth Analysis* for three, five and ten years. This enables investors to look at the best returns by individual shares over these three periods and then to find the stocks which have produced the best growth in earnings per share, dividends per share and net tangible assets per share over the same three periods.

From there, investors may crosscheck the current ratings of some of the better performers to see if there are some fast-growing stocks which have yet to be recognised by the stock market as a whole. One obvious way is to look at the current price/earnings ratio and dividend yield rankings.

Then there are other people who claim that looking for fast-growing stocks only leads investors astray and into buying shares in stocks which soar briefly, emit lots of sparkle like a rocket on Guy Fawkes night, only to splutter out and die. There is a body of opinion which says that the best way to select growth stocks for the long term is to look for shares which are selling on current dividend yields which are higher than average and which are priced on price/earnings ratios lower than average. These, it is argued, are the good value stocks and stocks selected on value and income often perform best in the medium to long term.

I am not aware of detailed surveys which prove or disprove this theory, and I have heard testimonies which suggest that this method sometimes produces unexpected growth stocks. Some of the fastest-growing stocks in terms of dividends in the last decade were not necessarily well-known or highly regarded stocks.

A quick crosscheck of the Statex figures suggests that using dividends per share growth rankings is slightly better than using earnings growth rankings. The stocks with the 20 fastest growths in earnings per share over the last decade coincided in 10 cases with the stocks producing the best return to investors. But, if you used those stocks with the fastest growth in dividends per share, the 20 best performers would have produced 12 of the 20 best-performing investments.

It is worth the time and effort for individual investors to scour the statistics — if that is your predilection — because finding the best performers can make a substantial difference to an individual investor's returns. Any of the 50 best-performing stocks over the last ten years would have produced individual returns which ranged from double to more than four times the average return per annum for the market as a whole. For instance, $1000 invested in the all ordinaries accumulation index would have risen over the decade to $2810. But, if it had been invested in the tenth best-performing stock, Westfield Holdings, the $1000 would have grown more than five times as fast to $18,402.

For the professionals handling portfolios worth billions of dollars, there are limited gains to be achieved by picking a share which performs exceptionally well. This does not mean they don't try to pick outperforming stocks but, because managers play the averages, they rarely have a very large exposure in one particular share in case it performs badly. They therefore also rarely gain from the occasional individual stock which outperforms everything in sight.

This is one aspect of investment in which the individual investor is different. If investors eschew the idea of investing in a listed or unlisted share trust, picking a winner or two is an important part of an individual investor's strategy since most people cannot afford to have more than five or six stocks in a portfolio. (In the 1991 ASX survey of shareowners, more than 47 per cent of all portfolios were worth $10,000 or less and about 53 per cent had only one or two stocks in the portfolio.)

The pessimists will say, of course, that this increases the odds of one of the shares performing badly. The optimists would see it in exactly the opposite light — one good performer can transform a small investor's returns.

But can we pick good performers by looking at their current price/earnings ratios and dividend yields? I did a study back in 1988, looking at the best-performing shares from 1985 to 1988 and studying their P/E ratios and dividend yields in 1985 at the start of the period. I wanted to find out if there was any discernible pattern in the P/E ratios in December 1985 which enabled investors to pick the winners.

The short answer is that there was no real pattern, perhaps because of the volatility in that period. The average 1985 P/E ratio on the top performers was 18.3 times, which of course was a high, even excessive multiple. But more than a quarter of the stocks were not showing a P/E ratio in 1985, a reflection of the number of emerging mining companies in the list. The exercise almost certainly needed to be conducted over more than three years because in two years after the survey period ended, five of the top 12 performers were off the list or in liquidation.

There were a few straws in the wind, though. Looking at those five failures, in 1985 they either had excessive P/E ratios (such as 66, 59 and 31 times earnings) or no figure at all because they were emerging from loss onto profits. And yet another industrial stock on the list which was selling at a P/E of 18 times last earnings — 50 per cent higher than the all-industrials average at the time of 11–12 times earnings — turned out to be the star share performer of the 1980s, BTR Nylex.

I also flirted with the theory that buying stocks with above-average dividend yields as well as low P/E ratios might produce good results. Once again the message was blurred; seven of the 25 best performers were selling on P/E ratios in 1985 that were below the market average, and four of these seven also in 1985 were on dividend yields above the market average. But BTR Nylex tended to contradict that, with a dividend yield well below the market average.

Even if I had taken the survey over a longer time period, I suspect that it would be difficult to produce real proof that picking stocks via low P/E ratios is an infallible system. The best we can say is that if the company is sound and its shares are selling on a below-average P/E ratio, investors should not come to too much trouble and, occasionally, just may pick a winner.

In many cases, however, investors may be checking out stocks from a working list which they or their adviser or stockbroker have selected. This is where even untutored investors can do some sensible sifting themselves.

Remember the sixth of our Ten Rules of Investment: understand what you are buying. For many people, this is perhaps the most important operating rule; you will feel more comfortable investing in an area in which you have some knowledge and it may help the investment pass the Sleep Test. But it is not much use sleeping at night, obliv-

GET TO KNOW THE COMPANY BEFORE YOU INVEST

ious to an unbalanced long-term portfolio which consists entirely of rental properties which, at critical times, could be disastrously illiquid. Nor is it any use investing in shares which your stockbroker feels comfortable with, but which you know nothing about.

The first thing investors should do to investigate a company they are considering is to telephone the company and seek a copy of the latest annual report. You should not worry about taking some time in this phase of the process, even if your stockbroker or adviser urges greater speed. If the stock has to be bought in a hurry, it is probably a speculation rather than an investment, anyway.

If it is a large company such as BHP or CSR, ask for the investor relations department; for smaller companies, it will usually be the share department or the company secretary who handles telephone inquiries. Tell the company you are an intending investor and would like annual reports for more than one year, as well as any additional information or reports that would be useful. If you sound like you know what you are doing and saying, you will be more likely to be given information; some companies try to limit the amount of information they mail to each caller just to reduce costs.

While you are about it, ask the company itself for details on how long they have paid ordinary dividends. This is a fairly basic piece of information which you will not readily get from any other source. Unlike the New York Stock Exchange which distributes brochures listing those companies with a long, uninterrupted dividend history, there is no easy way of obtaining this information in Australia (unless your stockbroker or adviser has a particular interest in the company).

As a matter of interest, BHP last missed an ordinary dividend in the Depression; there was a three-year gap between November 1929 and November 1932 when BHP shareholders had to go without dividends. Since then, BHP has been a model performer and the only time the dividend rate has been reduced since the Depression was in June 1942 in the Second World War when one dividend was trimmed, but since that time BHP has paid out an unchanged or higher dividend every year for over 50 years. CSR, which has a history of incorporation about as long as BHP's, has an even prouder record. It has not missed paying a dividend in any of its 103 years from 1888 and has earned a trading profit in every one of those years. Similarly, Coles Myer has never missed paying a dividend since it began as a public company in 1927 (as G.J. Coles). Of course, as this was just before the Depression there was not a very high dividend rate to start with, but the stock still has a 65-year history of paying a dividend. These are just three examples of companies which have paid dividends to shareholders without fail for decades.

While you are talking with the company representative, try to find out how the group's earnings are expected to turn out in the current year. Remember, much of the pricing of shares is based on expected earnings rather than on historical figures.

This is not an impossible task for the ordinary investor, though the large institutions do start off with an advantage in gathering this sort of information, but since the figures on likely earnings are available in the market place, small investors can obtain the information, as long as they ask.

It is certainly worth asking your stockbroker or adviser for their own forecasts of earnings or, in the case of a major company, whether he can give you what is called the Barcep figures for the company. Barcep is a service run by the Barclays group which produces a consensus figure of what stockbrokers' analysts expect for a company's profit, earnings and dividend per share for the current year and the next year. This service is too expensive for the average investor to buy, but many stockbrokers now subscribe and use the consensus figures in their in-house research.

If your stockbroker or adviser can't help, then ask the company involved. In most cases, if the company is keen about its shareholder relations, it will have the Barcep figures and, unless the figures show a potential disaster, it is likely that they give them to you. But you need to approach this question properly since companies are not allowed to tell you what they think the profit result may be (even if they know and even if they often give stockbrokers' analysts fairly broad hints). A company will generally provide the figures if you say something like: 'I'm keen to see whether the company can maintain its earnings this year. Can you tell me what the consensus figures are for stockbrokers' earnings estimates for the current year. And the dividend forecasts, too?'

When it comes to more detailed information on a company, I believe that ordinary investors ought to consider taking a close look in much the same way that they might inspect a house or other piece of real estate for sale. If the company's head office is in your own city and it's convenient, offer to call personally and collect the information instead of having it mailed to you. This gives you a chance to see the company's headquarters.

One rule arising from the excesses of the 1980s is to distrust companies with too much expensive marble in their foyers. As for companies with water fountains in their foyer, this is almost always a 'sell' rather than a 'buy' signal. Even if the office is in a city building, a visit may give you a clue on how the company is operated. If the office is at the company's main factory or operations centre, a visit may also give you a chance to see their property and get an idea of how the company is run.

You do not need to be a CIA agent to collect information on a plant visit. Get an impression of the building and its surrounds. Is it well-maintained? Are the staff cheerful or not? Is there an air of pride around the offices or building? Has the receptionist got a word processor or is she still struggling with a typewriter? If any company officer offers to give you as tour of the plant or factory, accept it immediately. Most journalists will tell you that you will always find out more about a company if you talk with an executive or manager on the factory floor rather than in their office.

ATTEND THE ANNUAL MEETING

The final suggestion is to find out when the company's annual meeting will be held. For most companies with a 30 June balance date, the usual 'season' for annual meetings is September to late November. For September balancing companies like the major banks, their annual meetings are usually in January, while BHP, as a May balancer, usually holds its annual meeting in September.

Annual meetings of many major companies are now grand occasions. They are often held in city hotels and can attract several hundred shareholders. They may show the latest corporate video or film or boast some additional presentations to shareholders apart from the normal business of an annual meeting.

Most importantly, though, the annual meetings provide a prospective shareholder with a chance to see the chairman and members of the board at first hand. I can always remember a disgusted shareholder at one company meeting some years ago where it was obvious that the company was on the skids. The shareholder had bought the shares on his stockbroker's recommendation and said to me: 'If I had seen those directors first, there is no way I would ever have bought these shares.' This was a case where it was more important to see the jockeys than to read the horse's form guide.

Finally, annual meetings give you a chance to meet directors afterwards or to collar a company executive to sound them out on facts about the company. Once again, you may find out more about a company over a cup of tea and a biscuit after the annual meeting than from all the statistical data a stockbroker's research report can deliver.

In particular, attend annual meetings held at the company's main plant; plant tours will often be given afterwards. Also, if the location is out of the way there may be fewer shareholders there. It is worth attending such a meeting for two reasons. The first and obvious one is that, with fewer shareholders, you have a better chance of talking with directors. The second is that some companies have been known to hold meetings at inconvenient times and at remote locations as a way of discouraging shareholders from attending and perhaps asking awkward questions. You should be aware of a company taking this approach.

Many people will regard annual meetings as a waste of time and doubt whether investors pick up any useful information from attending. My view is that annual meetings are designed to provide a forum for shareholders and you should take advantage of them, if possible. But, above all, they provide a perfect means of observing how a company operates and a chance to check what the board of directors looks like. Remember, you are buying shares in a company which is run by a board and executives, and anyone — whether a skilled analyst of balance sheets or not — is capable of making an assessment of people on a board.

I believe that most investors, if they had met Mr Alan

Jackson who turned BTR Nylex into the best-performing company on the Australian share list over the last decade, would have been impressed with his abilities. When there is an outstanding executive, it does not matter if the company is in a difficult or unfashionable area of operations. Similarly, anyone who had been involved with companies such as Gibson Chemicals or Brash Holdings over several decades would have had little difficulty in identifying enthusiastic chief executives who clearly knew what they were doing with their companies.

The late Victor Gibson of Gibson Chemicals was an ardent believer in communicating with shareholders and went to extraordinary lengths to attract shareholders to his annual meetings. Later, the present chairman, Mr Frank Lawson, took over this crusade and, more importantly, the successful concentration of the Gibson business on industrial and cleaning chemicals. I was impressed when I visited their plant more than 20 years ago, but it took the stock market (or the large institutions) almost another ten years to recognise Gibson. Since then, however, Gibson's record of increasing earnings and dividends has been reflected in its share price and in the ten years to the end of 1993 it produced total returns averaging 21.08 per cent compound a year to rank 72nd among all listed companies.

Similarly, I reported on Brash Holdings for more than 20 years. The most obvious asset of the company was its former managing director and chairman Geoff Brash. His family name clearly was no drawback in the company and there was no mistaking his enthusiasm and knowledge of the business. I can remember him surprising a newspaper photographer who, seeking a set-up for a photograph, asked Geoff Brash to sit at the keyboard of an organ. He did — and then proceeded to play it. Brash proved a remarkably resilient specialist retailer until the 1990s when it over-reached itself with diversification into book-selling. This cut back its 10-year performance from almost 27 per cent in the decade to 1991 to only 6.8 per cent in the 10 years to 1993.

The point about both Gibson and Brash is that anyone who had contact with their companies should have been able to recognise the leadership of the chief executives as an indication of the way the companies performed. It did not need a personal computer and a spreadsheet to come up with either of those investments; the normal ability to recognise people who knew what they were doing in their job would have been sufficient.

13

TIMING AND THE RIGHT STOCKS

Don't gamble; take all your savings and buy some good stock and hold it until it goes up, then sell it. If it doesn't go up, don't buy it.

— *American humorist, Will Rogers, on how to approach buying shares.*

A lot of the advice about how to buy good stocks and make money doing so tends to fall into the Will Rogers category. Everything will be okay if you exercise perfect hindsight. There is a danger that investors can be convinced of the fortunes to be made in the stock market by selecting a few examples of the real investment jackpots.

For example, any investor who managed to buy an obscure manufacturing company called BTR Hopkins in 1980 would, over the next ten years, have turned their original $100 into $1410 and would have picked up another $122 in dividend income in the ten years. That's the equivalent of earning more than 30 per cent compound a year for each of the ten years.

Some investors did achieve these sort of results from buying what is now BTR Nylex and is now among the ten largest Australian companies on the stock market list. But, between the end of 1979 and the end of 1989, they also could have turned their $100 into a total (including dividend income plus capital gain) of nearly $800 in Boral, more than $1200 in Pacific Dunlop and even more than $1000 in Elders IXL (before it became Foster's Brewing). These were the sort of leading industrial shares which many Australians would have routinely bought over the last 10 or 15 years.

Buy good stocks and sit on them; that seems to be the general idea. Well, yes, but as we saw earlier, it also takes timing. People might call BHP the best stock on the list, but there have been times when it has taken a long time to produce returns for someone who bought at the top of the market. Because it is now a large, diverse group, BHP will never produce the sort of growth in earnings which other, smaller companies can achieve, so it will be outrun in the growth stakes. Still, it has not done badly in recent years and in 1991, when there was concern about companies' dividend rates, BHP increased its dividend rate significantly.

As a matter of interest, over the three years to the end of 1993, BHP's return to investors (dividends and capital growth) was 24.12 per cent, which left it midway in the rankings though it beat shares such as MIM, Coles Myer, ANZ, Mayne Nickless and Boral. Over the five years to the end of 1993, BHP ranked 153rd among listed companies with its total return of 26.04 per cent. In the ten years to 1993, BHP improved on its 97th ranking for the decade to 1990 by coming in 48th place with a compound rate of growth of 23.4 per cent, well above the returns from bonds in the ten years.

Realistically, in the stock market there are no 'good' stocks or 'bad' stocks, only stocks which go up and stocks which go down. This means intending investors need the right approach to picking the right stocks.

It is possible to invest, long-term, in the stock market and to stick to the tried and true leading stocks on the list. These stocks can be top performers but they can also drift into dull periods. The difference between them and lesser stocks, however, is that major stocks can recover.

For instance, British Tobacco (Australia) turned itself from a purely tobacco company into the largest snack food company in Australia and has subsequently added the Coca-Cola business to its empire to regain its position as one of the leading stocks on the list. (It ranked 16th among all companies in the ten years to 1993 with a total return to investors of 31.68 per cent compound a year.)

CSR diversified several times into building materials and minerals with near-disastrous results when it went into oil, but managed to scramble out of its problems to become one of the largest building materials groups in Australia, as well as the major sugar company.

Investors can generally count on the large companies surviving a poor decision or two, but the smaller companies have fewer financial or management resources to fall back on in times of crisis. Thus if you like safety and don't mind sometimes sedate performance, then leading companies may be for you.

But many people want the best performance or, at least, better performance than the stock market on average. (If you are happy to take what the stock market does on average, there are several 'index funds' which invest in shares so that they virtually repeat the performance of the all ordinaries index. The MLC group, for instance, has one such publicly available fund.)

The search for growth means that people have to look for companies which will grow faster than many of the old faithful companies. For instance, despite the performance of BTR Nylex in the last ten years, in the three years from 1990 to 1993, 625 other companies on the list outperformed BTR Nylex's investor return of 11.94 per cent a year. Most of these were small companies (including some turnarounds of mining companies). But the fact remains that there are always new growth stocks emerging, and investors who like to seek out these sorts of stocks can make above-average gains, especially when the big investors are concentrating on the 50 or 100 largest companies.

PERSONAL APPROACHES TO SELECTING STOCK

So, when you look at how you are going to approach investment in the stock market, at a personal level it needs some honest assessment of your personality and approach to life. If you are an erratic person, prone to mood swings and to periods of self-confidence followed by self-doubt if something goes wrong, the stock market may not be the place for you. The stock market is not the best place to start discovering your character flaws.

First, you need to be certain what you are doing: you are approaching a market in which you want to invest to achieve long-term gains. If you want to speculate, stick to Lotto or, if you like the outdoor life, the racecourse. Never, ever, be seduced into chasing high returns on the basis that you need these high returns to produce an overall result above average. Be prepared to aim at returns after costs of 10–12 per cent or perhaps 5 per cent in real terms after inflation. If you cannot match inflation on your own over a couple of years then consider a managed investment where someone else does it for you.

Second, do not let your enthusiasm for the investment game get confused with love. Shares and companies are only pieces of paper and legal structures. Falling in love with a share is not a good idea. A stock market realist once said, 'Always remember, a share doesn't know you own it.' There are variations of this saying, including 'No matter what you think, the share doesn't owe you anything.' By all means study a few shares so that their characteristics and the way they move on the share market become familiar to you, but do not get into a one-way romance with a stock.

Third, try to get clear in your mind the sort of stocks you are looking at or buying. You may be content to buy only recognised leaders on the stock market, but beware of buying these stocks purely as a habit, at any price. You may prefer stocks which operate in an area you know and understand — for instance, if you work in the financial world, bank shares might be your specialty. But still beware of tunnel vision and remember to check how your shares stack up against the market as a whole. Or you might like to go fossicking for smaller companies which the big institutions so far have not discovered. There is nothing wrong with this approach, but you need to double-check everything because, if you make a mistake, there will not be the dozens of investment managers automatically buying the stock to help cover your mistake.

Fourth, research before you buy. People will spend weeks choosing their holiday destination and months selecting the right car, but they often spend only a few minutes on the telephone or in their stockbroker's office on an investment decision worth several times the cost of their annual holiday. But, you might complain, what if my stockbroker doesn't have research available on the stock? Well, at least ask for it, or ask if he can give you as copy of the ASX research service's material on the company. Or get a copy of the company's last couple of annual reports.

Finally, keep your wits about you. Ordinary investors

can pick up signals in the economy or particular industry as well as any institutional analyst, provided they keep their eyes and ears open and their mind engaged. It did not take a detailed knowledge of the commercial property market to see the coming glut in office space in Melbourne in 1990 and 1991. You did not need to be a financial analyst to get signals from the opulent lifestyle of Qintex Australia's Christopher Skase before the company collapsed.

DON'T FOLLOW THE BIG MANAGERS

How can you select the right stock at the right time? Definitely not by following what the biggest investment managers are doing. Most of the time, they are 'weighting' their portfolio according to the index which means they are really just doing what everyone else is doing, with a few variations. ('Weighting' means holding roughly the same percentage in particular stocks as the stocks represent in the all ordinaries index or whatever other index the managers hope to 'track'.)

Professional fund managers have investments in their funds other than shares, in any case, and many of the largest funds have shares at such low average costs that they don't have to worry about whether they are buying at the right time. Finally, you only discover what the big players are doing after they have acted. Investment managers, such as the large life offices, which run funds with billions of dollars are not going to tip you off before they buy or sell.

Perhaps, as an alternative, the small investor should buy what the institutions are selling and vice versa? This generally can be a mistake over the short term since the institutions' dealings tend to make the market. But the best time to buy may still be when other holders are selling — provided you are sure of the long-term prospects of the company.

How do you know that? Past performance is one sign — for instance, how many years has the company paid a dividend? Has it ever had to reduce the dividend or omit payment? What has been its growth (capital and dividends) in recent years? In many cases, your stockbroker or adviser should be able to tell you this; for three-year returns you can get an indication of performance from the Australian Stock Exchange Journal which shows each month the performance of $1000 if held over one year and three years. A quick glance down these columns will quickly identify the fast-growers. The same material, in more detail and covering five and ten years, is available from the ASX research department.

You can even convert figures like $1000 growing in three years to $1597 into an annual compound rate of return simply by using an old-fashioned set of growth tables. In this case, the answer is about 16.9 per cent a year compound and the stock which has performed this well in less than buoyant times is in fact one of those listed investment trusts, the Adelaide-based Argo Investment. Australian Foundation Investment Co has done even better, with $1000 turning into $1835 in three years — a 22.4 per cent a year growth rate.

Apart from seeking those stocks which have grown rapidly in the past, how do you chose those which are likely to produce good results in the future? If we assume that earnings are the key to future growth, then investors need to be able to identify those companies which will produce above-average profit growth. This is crystal ball country and, while a few shrewd analysts may be able to identify some of the fast-growers, the number of potential candidates on the stock exchange list is too large for the average investor to tackle.

ODDS-ON OR EACH-WAY?

That means you have to adopt some of the techniques of the professional investors and sift through the list with some sort of objective criteria to sort the wheat from the chaff. My general view is that you can do two things: bet on the odds-on chances or look for better value among the each-way bets.

If you like betting on favourites, then you look at the leading stocks selling on relatively high price/earnings ratios and on low dividend yields. These are the stocks which investors have decided are worth paying more for. You are betting that most investors are right and that the stock is going to win, even at short odds. Some people don't mind following the popular money, and it has to be said that if you adopt this approach, you will be among some esteemed company.

But you also may have to be prepared for the occasional

disappointment. For instance, people bought News Corporation shares in 1990 on a dividend yield of less than 1 per cent when they were $12–14. The shares then fell to as low as $3.19 (yield 3.1 per cent) and then trebled in price to $9 (yield 1.1 per cent). The theory on very low dividend yields is that the share price rises to compensate you for the lack of immediate dividend, but long-term holders of News had their patience sorely tested for a time. However, those that rode the trend through hit the jackpot with growth averaging just under 100 per cent in each of the three years to 1993.

In general terms, the odds-on stocks do offer good past form in the growth stakes for the low yields. For instance stocks such as BHP, Brickworks, QBE, Soul Pattinson and George Weston, which all yield less than 4 per cent from their dividends, have all achieved capital growth of 20 to 28 per cent a year in the last ten years.

The best-performing shares in terms of dividend growth also have been among the best performers in total growth which, on reflection, should not be surprising, but the interesting thing is that of the best performers on this dividend measure, only a minority of the top performers of ten years ago would have been an automatic selection as a leading share. Lend Lease and perhaps Boral would have qualified and yet some of the companies which were more obscure ten years ago — such as BTR Nylex, Wesfarmers, Renison Gold Fields and SA Brewing — have produced outstanding growth in dividends and total returns. There is a clear message here: investors should cast their net beyond the established names to look for future growth.

So, if investors have identified stocks which have provided good growth and returns in the past, the next trick is to decide whether these stocks can achieve future growth.

That can depend largely on an assessment of whether growth in the share price has run too far ahead of growth in earnings and dividends. Once again, this is a case of seeking the relevant growth rates from your stockbroker or adviser: the growth in dividends per share, earnings per share and the share price.

If the three rates have tended to match each other (or, more promisingly, if share price growth appears to have been lagging the company's actual earnings and dividend performance) then investors have to sit down and look at the company to assess whether it can sustain past growth in the future.

RESEARCHING THE COMPANY

At this point, investors should remember that they are not buying a share or a mere price in a table of share prices, but a share in a company which employs thousands of people to make or sell goods or services. This is where the amateur investor needs to start doing some detective work. What industry is the company in? Is this a growing, mature or declining industry? The answer may not be so important if the company is a leader in its industry and is increasing its share of the market.

Do the company's products have a niche in the market? A building contractor may face a lot of competition but a company like Lend Lease in the large-scale development field has a reputation and name which will help it over rough patches and keep it in front of competitors. Companies like CSR and Boral have strong positions in the building materials field — no-one is going to bring blue metal from interstate to compete with Boral or import bricks from overseas to undercut CSR.

WHAT YOU CAN FIND OUT FROM THE ANNUAL REPORT

The next checkpoint is the financial strength of the company. There is no easy way around this; you will just have to look at a balance sheet. This may be a less daunting task than you imagine. In any case, there are other bonuses to be gained in this exercise since, strange as it may seem, many people invest in companies without ever looking at their annual report and balance sheet.

Many investors baulk at looking at annual reports. There is a story, no doubt apocryphal, about one public company which thought it would save money. Instead of mailing dividend cheques and annual reports separately, it enclosed the dividend cheques inside the annual reports. The company had never had so many complaints about delays in the mail and lost dividend cheques — hundreds of shareholders had thrown away their cheques with the unopened annual reports.

Annual reports are designed to give information. In fact, they have evolved into their present form as a result of decades of demands for more information. Now, the full annual report is often too much for the average shareholder to digest and they are offered, instead, a condensed version of the accounts. For the serious investor, however, the annual report is a major source of information about any company.

But how does a prospective investor obtain a company annual report before buying the shares? Your stockbroker or adviser may have one to spare but in most cases the simplest method is to telephone the company and ask the investor relations officer or company secretary for a copy by mail. Most companies now regard their annual report as a part of their overall marketing operations and are glad to distribute copies. While you are in touch with the company, try your luck and ask for the last three annual reports and a copy of any other reports or information sent to shareholders in the last 12 months.

That should help you in two ways: firstly, it gives you a base of information about the company going back perhaps three or four years (or a decade if the company includes a ten-year table of important information in its report), and secondly, it gives you a chance to assess how the company regards and treats its shareholders. You can learn a lot from the way a company handles inquiries from the public or shareholders, and the way it communicates with investors; many of the larger companies now have very good investor relations departments which are geared to provide virtually everything a potential or existing shareholder wants. You may, of course, learn in a third way; if the company refuses to provide information or cannot help, you ought to reconsider whether you are interested in buying its shares (except, perhaps, as a takeover prospect!).

The important thing to look for in a company's balance sheet is the level of borrowings or 'gearing' as it has become the fashion to describe borrowings. Many companies calculate a gearing ratio in their table of comparative figures. For instance, the 1993 Amcor annual report shows this in a five-year statistics table, reproduced in part overleaf.

The level of gearing is usually expressed as a ratio of total borrowings to shareholders' funds; this gives a debt-to-equity ratio. The Amcor ratio of term loan funds to shareholders' funds is effectively the same measure. A level of 50 per cent or less is a fairly conservative gearing level. Anything above 100 per cent — that is, total borrowings equal to or greater than shareholders' funds — is a warning sign. Such a level may be only an isolated instance and the company may subsequently reduce this level, but persistent levels of borrowings at or above the level of shareholders' funds or total tangible assets points to one important thing: if it comes to a crunch, the company's lenders own more of the company than do the shareholders.

I will always remember my first lesson in assessing companies' borrowings. During the 1960s crashes, the then chief executive of Lend Lease, Dick Dusseldorp, told how his company had dozens of competitors who wanted him to acquire them. He would look at the balance sheet, compare the size of their borrowings to their shareholders' funds and tell them: 'It's no good talking to me. Go and talk to your lenders because they really own you.'

The figure for shareholders' funds or total tangible assets produces one other significant number for investors: divide this figure by the number of issued shares and you have the net asset backing per share. This shows how much, in theory, each shareholder would own if the company was wound up and the proceeds distributed. It is also a shorthand way of calculating what the company may be worth to a potential acquirer. In addition, the ratio of the share market price to the net asset backing figure is also a quick way of judging whether the share market thinks highly of the company or not.

These days, with most companies using fairly up-to-date valuations in their accounts, the net asset backing figure ought to be reasonably indicative of the company's real worth. If you suspect the assets are undervalued, a look through the notes to the accounts will disclose the date of valuation of major assets. In addition, the statement of accounting policies often will tell you how often directors value assets. If the stock market is pricing the shares above the net asset backing, this usually indicates that investors are happy to pay a premium above the apparent book value of the company for the group's past record, the expertise of the board and management and for other intangibles

AMCOR STATISTICS

For years ended 30 June		1993	1992	1991	1990	1989	1988
(Results shown before abnormal items except where indicated)							
Consolidated Results:							
Net sales	($000)	4,824,594	4,111,600	3,342,826	3,250,606	2,209,326	1,783,444
Operating profit before interest & tax	($000)	509,794	473,351	405,611	356,718	292,524	250,388
Operating profit before tax	($000)	434,595	357,841	249,605	196,429	190,737	174,685
Net operating profit	($000)	266,944	223,105	172,384	143,055	139,023	111,365
Net operating profit after abnormals	($000)	314,897	266,480	229,238	166,220	131,723	120,372
Earnings per share	*(cents)	49.7	44.3	35.5	32.8	36.8	30.9
Return on shareholders' funds	(% p.a.)	11.7	11.2	9.6	9.2	11.7	11.7
Dividend	($000)	169,400	148,132	122,629	117,577	96,003	78,041
Dividend per ordinary share	(cents)	31.0	29.0	27.0	27.0	26.5	21.4
Dividend franking	(%p.a.)	100.0	80.0	55.2	69.8	81.5	79.1
Dividend cover	(times)	1.58	1.51	1.41	1.22	1.45	1.43
Financial Ratios							
Net tangible asset backing per share	($)	3.58	3.30	3.15	3.01	3.37	3.37
Net interest cover	(times)	6.8	4.1	2.6	2.2	2.9	3.3
Gearing (shareholders' funds: term loan funds)	(ratio)	74:26	72.28	68.32	63.37	63.37	63.37
Liabilities/assets	(%)	43	47	47	52	51	50
Current asset ratio	(times)	1.77	1.52	1.47	1.22	1.42	1.44
Financial Statistics							
Income from dividends and interest	($000)	32,656	42,512	50,717	52,070	50,931	43,409
Depreciation and amortisation provided during year	($000)	191,106	162,421	140,480	121,555	85,228	68,181
Net interest	($000)	75,199	115,510	156,006	160,289	101,787	75,703
Cash flow from operations	($000)	433,394	394,461	278,537	212,386	178,960	160,048
Capital expenditure & acquisitions	($000)	708,000	355,000	300,000	660,000	494,000	400,000
Balance Sheet Data as at 30 June							
Current assets	($000)	1,638,370	1,416,316	980,596	1,002,562	805,351	616,499
Non-current assets	($000)	3,367,771	2,935,256	2,837,744	2,886,388	2,289,899	1,857,749
Total Assets		5,006,141	4,351,572	3,818,340	3,888,950	3,095,250	2,474,248
Current liabilities	($000)	925,199	929,303	665,450	820,908	566,935	428,116
Non-current liabilities	($000)	1,249,079	1,114,172	1,124,616	1,213,836	1,007,739	821,694
Total Liabilities		2,174,278	2,043,475	1,790,066	2,034,744	1,574,674	1,249,810
Net Assets		2,831,863	2,308,097	2,028,274	1,854,206	1,520,576	1,244,438
Shareholder's Funds							
Share capital	($000)	573,229	514,126	492,962	469,918	389,522	333,900
Reserves	($000)	1,426,044	1,065,111	968,295	925,756	682,471	538,214
Retained profits	($000)	601,748	456,321	390,789	283,529	234,585	222,016
Shareholders' funds attributable to parent entity	($000)	2,601,021	2,035,558	1,852,046	1,679,203	1,306,578	1,094,130
Outside equity interests in controlled entities	($000)	**130,959**	136,083	11,566	5,778	1,220	308

AMCOR STATISTICS

For years ended 30 June (Results shown before abnormal items except where indicated)		1993	1992	1991	1990	1989	1988
Undated subordinated convertible securities	($000)	99,883	136,456	164,662	169,225	212,778	130,000
Total Shareholders' Funds		2,831,863	2,308,097	2,028,274	1,854,206	1,520,576	1,244,438
Amcor Equity Results:							
Net sales	($000)	5,078,571	4,381,953	4,394,660	4,372,515	3,499,260	2,899,919
Net operating profit	($000)	268,983	223,804	169,353	156,408	161,953	137,132
Net operating profit after abnormals	($000)	321,536	267,179	227,665	180,959	150,877	146,886
Other Data as at 30 June							
Issued shares	($000)	578,951	520,076	494,303	471,453	391,185	335,164
Amcor share price:							
year's high	($)	8.64	7.72	5.50	5.10	5.40	6.30
year's low	($)	7.22	5.20	3.46	3.91	4.00	2.60
close	($)	7.99	7.62	5.36	4.31	4.15	4.74
Employee numbers		18,100	18,000	16,700	17,700	18,00	12,700
Number of shareholders		71,000	65,000	54,000	52,000	48,000	46,000

*Based on net operating profit before abnormals divided by the time-weighted average number of shares on issue.

which may not have a value put on them in the balance sheet. If the shares are selling below net asset backing, this suggests that the company is not as highly valued by the stock market. It may also indicate, when other conditions are ripe, that takeover bidders might emerge who think they can better use the assets.

In general terms, there is now more than enough information in a company annual report to keep the average investor browsing for hours — the Amcor 1993 report, for instance, ran to 64 pages, almost half of which consisted of the detailed financial figures and statistics. The things to look for are the broad picture of borrowings and net assets and other trends which may emerge in the handy long-term performance tables.

For many smaller companies, there may be less detail provided in the annual report than is given by the major companies. Investors should read the reports with a sceptical eye; glossy sales or marketing oriented reports are a danger sign, especially if this coincides with an over-geared balance sheet or a confused picture of what the company does. Remember that shrewd investor in Chapter 5 who would not buy a share unless he could understand the balance sheet and see where the company earned its profits? This is where even an untutored investor can glean some important impressions.

Look at the directors report and the profit and loss account. Where did the profit come from? Was it mostly from sales? Or did investments or other non-trading items produce large earnings? Was the income tax provision about normal or did the company benefit from deductions which might not necessarily be available in the future? If all else fails, ask yourself: 'Can I understand where this company made most of its profits?'

The emphasis we put on borrowings in discussing the balance sheet was a direct lesson from the 1987 crash when over-borrowed companies became unacceptable and, in many cases, went into oblivion. The second lesson from 1987 and afterwards, however, is that the stock market and investors now want uncomplicated companies. They do not like a group which featured complex, inter-company holdings such as those of John Spalvins and his Adelaide Steamships group.

So investors need to look at company accounts and see whether its structure is easy to follow. Is it part of another group? (Check in the back of the annual report to identify the major shareholders.) Where does the company sit in an overall corporate structure? Does it depend on other members of the group?

No one should put down a company annual report without reading the auditor's report. Finance journalists, who might handle dozens of annual reports at a time, routinely look at the auditor's report just in case there are some qualifications. This may be a over-cynical approach but investors ignore auditor's reports at their peril.

Finally, investors should look at the board of directors and the senior management as listed in the annual report. This lists their length of service on the board and their other qualifications. In many cases, the board and executives may be well-known people. If you don't know anything about them, ask your financial adviser for an opinion on them. Are they known performers? What is their reputation?

Many times, when potential investors ask me what is the key factor to consider in choosing an investment, I remind them that they are backing the jockey as well as the horse in the investment stakes. The board of directors and senior management team is perhaps the single most important factor in the success of a company. If they are experienced and competent they will manage the company well and produce good returns for investors.

The name and reputation of directors is a fairly good gauge of the quality of the company since the responsibilities of directors now ensure that the better directors will only join boards where they have confidence in the company and their fellow directors. If a board consists of unknown directors, if it is dominated by executive directors or if the chief executive or chairman is the largest shareholder, investors ought to keep a careful eye on things.

This is only the bare outline of what investors can learn from a company annual report and balance sheet, but it covers the essentials for any investor contemplating investing in a company.

14

HELP!

A broker is someone who invests other people's money until it is all gone.

— *Woody Allen, no doubt talking about New York stockbrokers*

*T*his chapter was originally to be entitled 'All those boring things you need to know about investment which we are putting at the back of the book.' The new title is recognition, however, that investment — even for the professionals — is a case of relying on other people for help.

It was put last for a particular reason: the aim of *The Art of Investment* is to emphasise the positives of investing, particularly in shares, rather than to bog down the reader in discussions on choosing a stockbroker or other financial adviser, or in the complexities of financial planning, superannuation, rollovers, capital gains tax and so on. All these subjects are important and cannot be ignored by most investors, but they are part of the technicalities of investment and the important thing for investors is to get the essential things into perspective first.

An understanding and helpful stockbroker or financial adviser can make investment a less stressful business. But the long-term success of an investor, in the end, will depend much more on the passing of time and patience in investing, rather than in the intrinsic qualities of an adviser. This is not meant to denigrate the role of a stockbroker or financial adviser. The right one, with the necessary backup services, can be an invaluable ally in any investor's program. The potential harm which can be caused by a wrong adviser is substantial. This means that the choice of an adviser or stockbroker should be undertaken in the same way as the rest of the approach to long-term investment — carefully and after a great deal of thinking and research.

Many people think a personal introduction is needed to see a stockbroker, but this is unnecessary. What is needed is some way of matching the client to the broker. For instance, if you approach the introduction service run by the stock exchanges in each capital city, the service will ask several questions designed to identify the sort of investor you are and the services you need.

In general, the stock exchange people will ask you how much money you have to invest and whether you require services which might generally be called financial planning. The range of services offered by stockbrokers can vary widely. Some offer a full service, ranging across all types of investments, including financial planning for clients and retirement investment advice and services. If you want a total package, the introduction service will steer you towards a stockbroker offering these services.

If you have a large amount of money to invest (the average is around $20,000 but do not be intimidated if you have much less), the service may give you an introduction to a stockbroker who specialises in handling larger amounts. But there is no guaranteed way of matching broker and client on a personal level, other than the two parties meeting and talking. Unless you have an introduction from someone who understands your needs and you find an understanding stockbroker, do not be frightened to shop around a little via interviews before settling on your final choice.

While the stockbrokers might not admit as much publicly, a good base of private clients is starting to look much less of a liability than it did a few years ago. Then, the conventional wisdom among stockbrokers was that small clients were too expensive to service, basically because it could take longer to deal with a small client investing only $5000 than with an institution investing $5 million.

But, after dozens of existing and new stockbroking firms

FINDING A STOCKBROKER

all set out to woo the institutional investor, this sector of the market became overcrowded. A few leading broking firms are emerging, with varying strengths in areas such as research, market-making, options and futures trading and so on. But brokers without a particular strength find it hard to get institutional orders.

MODERN TRADING SYSTEMS

In the last year or so, there have been two near-revolutions in the stockbroking field: FAST and SEATS. FAST (Flexible Accelerated Security Transfer system) essentially eliminates the holding of physical share certificates. This enables the transfer system to work much more quickly by eliminating the delays caused by various parties in each transaction exchanging pieces of paper. Generally, FAST is currently used mainly by the larger investors in the major companies which have joined this system. But it is likely to spread to all securities, ahead of the ultimate reform of the system, involving completely paperless share transfers promised by the so-called CHESS system (Clearing House Electronic Subregister System) which is due to be phased in from September 1994.

SEATS (Stock Exchange Automated Trading System) is the computer-driven trading system which has replaced the traditional trading floor. It allows much quicker and more economical trading of shares and small orders from private clients can be handled much more economically.

The combination of these improvements to the share trading system means that costs of share trading are coming down. If costs can be reduced further by these systems, then private clients will become a more attractive side of the business for stockbrokers, so don't assume that stockbrokers are doing you a favour by taking you as a client.

Many first-time investors fear that they will be merely one of the small fry in the large sweep of clients in a stockbroker's office. The trick is to find the right balance between a broking firm which is small enough to give personalised attention but large enough to offer the sort of additional services you might like, such as regular research reports and client letters. The final choice must be up to each individual investor because, above all, you need to like the stockbroking adviser you will be dealing with and you need to trust the integrity of the firm.

Much the same remarks apply to shopping for a financial adviser who is not a stockbroker. In general, these advisers may be more specialised for areas of financial advice such as retirement and pre-retirement planning, the investment of superannuation lump sums, the purchase of annuities and the establishment of a total financial plan. The problem in this area is not in the ranks of the larger and reputable organisations but in the wide variety of possible financial advisers that a first-time investor may encounter.

OTHER FINANCIAL ADVISERS

You may find an adviser who charges little or no fees but he will almost certainly be receiving his commissions from investment managers who market the products in which you invest. You may find an adviser who rebates up to five per cent of his commissions, but who charges a fee for service. This seems to be more the trend these days and it is certainly an approach which is less susceptible to pressures on the manager to recommend investments simply because of the level of commission they pay.

You also may find yourself dealing with a life insurance company agent or, occasionally, the sales agent of another group which is trading as a financial adviser. These groups may well offer good service, but there is a danger that they will recommend investments which favour their own field or company. When dealing with insurance salesmen, remember that they are agents and will be paid even higher commission than a financial adviser recommending a similar product.

When it comes to share investments and most of the managed investment products produced for the retail market, advisers — whether they are stockbrokers or financial planners — have a statutory duty under the securities legislation to ensure that the investments they recommend to you are suitable for your needs. It is known, in the trade shorthand as the 'know your client' rule and it is to the advantage of an investor to allow their adviser to get to know them as closely as possible.

In all cases, you should treat the first interview as the one where both parties put their cards on the table. You should

MEETING YOUR ADVISER

talk frankly of your aims and resources, and about any doubts you may have about some aspects of investments. You should expect a comprehensive review from the potential adviser on how the firm operates, how it charges and what the level of fees is likely to be. You should expect explanations in a language you can understand. Don't allow an adviser to baffle you with phrases you cannot understand or which are not explained.

These days, times are competitive in both the financial advice and the stockbroking businesses, so you should expect a welcoming approach from your potential adviser. You should be able to talk frankly about the fees and charges. Most brokers levy a 2.5 per cent commission (or a minimum charge) up to a level of $5000 of business. But many stockbroking advisers are prepared to be flexible on rates if it means they get your business, so an order of around $50,000, depending on the size of the broking house, could see the broker prepared to reduce the brokerage rates.

These days, investment life is complicated so there are obvious advantages in finding an adviser who can handle most of the other messy parts of the process. You will find that most advisers, whether stockbrokers, accountants or financial planners, will be well aware of the taxation and other implications of the investment choices they are presenting to you. But beware of anyone who presses an investment merely or mainly because of its taxation advantages. This sort of investment proliferates especially around the end of the tax year. The average person should avoid them, since they are usually aimed at people on the top tax bracket who have enough money to 'buy' a tax deduction. All investments should be worthwhile in their own right and any tax advantage should be seen very much as an incidental bonus.

TAXATION WORRIES

Now, what about the drawbacks of direct investment? Surely it's complicated and presents a nightmare task in recording transactions and keeping the details for the tax man? Perhaps, but the drawbacks are nowhere near sufficient to stop you investing.

More and more financial advisers and stockbrokers are offering a computerised service which records and tracks your portfolio. If record-keeping is not your strong point, make sure your broker or adviser offers such a service (and does not charge for it). It enables you to get regular reports on your investments (usually quarterly) and makes the task of getting an immediate valuation very easy. Such systems usually deliver to you or to your accountant all the necessary information at income tax time.

Now, capital gains tax. The taxation system can be fiendishly complicated but, once again, you can take advantage of the services of the experts. If you can make a success of long-term investment, the fear of paying capital gains tax is the least of your worries. (Remember, there is indexation of the cost base to allow for inflation and ease the burden a little.) Your financial adviser or stockbroker should be able to handle the necessary record-keeping, in addition to what you might do for your own purposes. But a fear of capital gains tax or annoyance at having to pay tax on gains is no reason to shy away from a long-term investment program.

Superannuation is a topic sufficient to fill another book. It should be part of everyone's long-term financial plans and you should aim to be in a scheme in which your employer pays part of the contributions. The more you can accumulate and get invested, the better chance of having a reasonable sum on which to retire. If you have a good superannuation scheme with generous contributions by your employer and few worries at retirement, then you should be thankful.

Many people, however, will have little superannuation or an inadequate amount. No-one, for instance, should count on the three per cent (planned to rise to nine per cent by the year 2003) industry funds now operating. Even for relatively young workers, such funds are unlikely to provide a lump sum of much more than one or two years' final salary on retirement. For many people, the idea of superannuation is unattractive, largely because the money is locked away and untouchable until late in life. People in this situation are probably the ones who should look most closely at an alternative long-term investment approach, such as we have been suggesting in *The Art of Investment*.

SUPERANNUATION

Questions relating to retirement planning, such as rollover of superannuation lump sums or the strategies of using annuities for retirement income, are all best approached through a financial adviser or planner. In general, all areas of finance — accounting, taxation, superannuation, annuities and retirement planning — have become so complex that you should rely largely on the advice of experts.

Any general investment book will be able only to give the most general advice and you should shop around for more detailed books. There are now a large number of explanatory books on retirement planning, superannuation, rollovers and annuities available from specialist book shops, from organisations like the Life Insurance Federation of Australia and the Association of Superannuation Funds of Australia, or from investment managers. As with all investments, shop around.

THE ART OF INVESTMENT

Perhaps I can summarise *The Art of Investment*:

Not only is investment important for your future, it is also possible for the ordinary person to participate in it.

Investment can be as complicated or as simple as you want to make it. There can be many tests of a share investment but in the end it comes down to a well-run company doing what it knows best.

Above all, investors are backing the jockey rather than the horse and should rely on their own judgment of people.

Finally, if investors keep their eyes open and follow a few sensible rules, they have as good a chance as the professionals of achieving good results.

American investment guru of the 1970s and 1980s, Howard Ruff, tells the story of a woman who, when he was giving advice, interrupted him and said, 'But I don't know anything about investment.'

Ruff replied succinctly: 'Don't worry, ignorance is a curable disease.'

This book is dedicated to that simple proposition.

Appendix

INFORMATION SOURCES

Investors and potential investors now have an increasing number of sources of information available to them. The important thing is to know where to look; hence this appendix which is designed to provide a working list of sources of information.

ASX SERVICES

The major source of information on investment and the stock market in particular is the Australian Stock Exchange (ASX). There are bookshops or investor centres at all the state exchanges. All these offer the ASX range of books and information and many of them also stock a very wide range of other investment, financial and general business books. The ASX also offers a mail order service for much of its detailed information. In addition, investors can seek information from a Customer Service Centre on 008 029 962.

The backbone of the ASX research operation for decades has been the so-called Red Book service, now called the Company Review Service which provides detailed information, updated regularly, on every listed company. The full service costs more than $10,000 a year and is bought mainly by stockbrokers, institutions and newspapers. The service is also available on a compact disk for computers users. For small investors, however, individual company copies are available at $11.95 per copy (plus postage and handling).

The other ASX research material available is, in summary:

- The Statex service — financial and performance statistics on listed companies. Most of these are designed for stockbrokers and investment and financial analysts but they provide useful figures on individual companies and also comparative figures for both companies and indices.

  For instance, a study is available regularly giving investor return figures and growth analysis over three, five and ten years for all listed companies. It lists the companies by returns and then alphabetically. This costs $70 for a single copy.

  The Statex service also offers share price charts and printouts, covering share prices over a maximum of 20 years (at $20 for the first company and $10 for each additional one).

- Market data — this is aimed mainly at stockbrokers and institutional investors and covers major announcements by companies, stock market quotations, and other market detail.

- Index information service — this offers in-depth detail on local and overseas indices, aimed mainly at professional investors and stockbrokers. The *Weekly Index Analysis* provides a lot of market information. A single copy costs $15 and a weekly subscription $520.

- Annual stock market summaries — these can be useful for tax purposes, giving end-of-year closing prices, calls paid, bonuses issues, rights issues and prices, dividends paid, delistings, takeovers and company reconstructions and dividend imputation details.

- A more detailed listing of products and services is available from the ASX by calling 008 029 962.

REFERENCE BOOKS   There are several useful reference books now produced for the smaller investor. One is the ASX's publication, the *All Ordinaries Index Companies Handbook* (295pp, $38.95). This covers more than 270 companies on the all ordinaries index and has a compact, one-page listing for each company. It also gives detailed information on how the AOI is constructed and calculated.

Investors using this and other books should note that the stocks in the indices (and thus in the books) are chosen on measurable criteria (such as market capitalisation and level of activity) and there is no qualitative assessment involved in a stock being included in an index.

A companion book, *Australia's Top 100*, covers the 100 largest companies by market capitalisation and costs $19.95. Both books bring together information not otherwise found in one place, such as the company board and management, telephone numbers, etc.

For the more serious investor the ASX publishes *The Yearbook* (cost $275) which covers all 1050 companies on the ASX.

Another good resource is *The Australian Financial Review Shareholder* (cost $44.95) which gives details of the top 500 listed companies. It includes, as well as the top 500 companies, a supplementary list of other companies, notes on brokerage, stamp duty and a list of stockbrokers. A sample page from the *Shareholder* appears as Table A.

The following gives further sources for the types of information covered in the various chapters of this book. The tables referred to appear in order at the end of the appendix.

USEFUL SOURCES CHAPTER BY CHAPTER

- **Chapter 1:**

Long-term rates of return. In addition to the long-term returns statistics referred to in the book, there is a variety of sources for such returns. One regular study is that undertaken by the Association of Superannuation Funds of Australia (AFSA), which produces annual figures on long-term real rates of return. Table B, which summarises the latest figures for a number of different periods, was published in the March 1994 issue of ASFA's magazine *Superfunds*.

As noted in this book, investors should aim at achieving real rates of return above the level of inflation. This table shows that this has not always been easy over periods up to 10 years, although most 20-year periods studied and all 25-year periods have seen superannuation funds match or beat inflation.

- **Chapter 2:**

Decline in the value of the dollar. Table C following is prepared regularly by J.B. Were & Son to show the potential loss of purchasing power of the dollar. It is normally updated annually.

- **Chapter 3:**

Shares versus debentures. J.B. Were & Son produces annual study of returns from a portfolio of typical leading shares and a corporate debenture, the A.G.C. debenture. See table D.

- **Chapter 8:**

Dividend imputation: ANZ McCaughan produces a handbook called *The Australian Dividend Handbook* (cost $25) which includes details of dividend imputation and tables prepared by chartered accountants Coopers & Lybrand. See Table E

- **Chapter 12:**

Long-term returns. The Statex service of the ASX produces long-term return figures, as outlined earlier. Table G is an example of the information it provides on the performance of stocks. This extract from an investor returns publication shows the best performing stocks over the 10 years to December 1993, indicating the growth of $1000 invested and the compound rate of growth per annum.

The calculation of investor returns includes all capital gains in the shares and dividends paid over the period. Bonus shares are held and added to the holding. In cases of rights issues, the rights are theoretically sold on the first day of rights trading and the proceeds invested in the ordinary shares. Dividends are assumed to be reinvested in the shares at the month-end price after the shares go ex-dividend. The returns do not allow for any brokerage fee.

Long-term returns on the All Ordinaries Index. Armstrong Jones produces a detailed analysis of share market trends and returns which is available as a wall chart from the fund managers at the following locations:

Level 21, Royal Exchange Building
56 Pitt Street
Sydney NSW 2000
Tel: (02) 250 2000, (008) 226 236
Fax: (02) 221 6152

Level 10, Australia Place
15 William Street
Perth WA 6000
Tel: (09) 322 0141, (008) 998 064
Fax: (09) 481 1859

Level 5, Armstrong Jones Centre
580 St Kilda Road
Melbourne Vic 3004
Tel: (03 529 1999, (008) 033 002
Fax: (03) 521 2421

Level 2, 500 Queen St
Brisbane Qld 4000
Tel: (07) 831 7066
Fax: (07) 834 5010

TABLE A: SAMPLE PAGE FROM THE AUSTRALIAN FINANCIAL REVIEW SHAREHOLDER

THE BROKEN HILL PROPRIETARY COMPANY LIMITED

Mining, Oil and Gas, Steel

Market Cap ($m) : 29,614.9
ASX Code : BHP
Y/E : 31 May

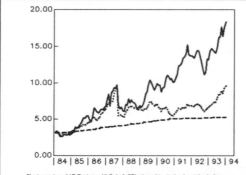

Charts courtesy AAP Reuters. All Ords & CPI rebased to stock price at beginning.
Graph lines: Solid = Company   Dashes = CPI   Dots = A/O Index

EVENTS IN REPORTING PERIOD

- Profit attributable to BHP shareholders increased by 27.5% to $640m.
- Highest half yearly raw steel production for 14 years.
- Earnings per share at 47.9c per share up 22.2%.
- Outlook In the medium to longer term developments underway and planned will continue to grow shareholder value. Profit outlook is sensitive to international commodity prices and these are currently at depressed levels. These prices will make it difficult to maintain the improved profit performance in the second half of this current year. BHP businesses in general are operating at capacity with demand for most products continuing to remain firm. Mr BT Loton, Chairman of Directors, 17 Dec 1993.

NATURE OF BUSINESS

BHP Minerals explores, develops and produces coking and thermal coals, iron ore, copper, concentrates, manganese, gold, titanium, nickel, zinc–lead concentrates and ferroalloys from operations in 28 countries and sells to customers worldwide.

Main Controlled Entities include Australian Iron & Steel Pty Ltd   BHP Holdings (USA) Inc   BHP (USA) Investments Inc   BHP Minerals International Hamilton Oil Company Inc   Beswick Pty Ltd   BHP Petroleum International BHP Petroleum (NW Shelf) Pty Ltd   BHP Australia Coal Ltd   BHP Minerals Ltd   Pilbara Iron Ltd   BHP Transport Ltd   John Lysaght (Australia) Ltd.

Half Year Revenue Segments :
Business ($m) Petroleum 2,317.2   Minerals 2,374.8   Steel 3,459.7
Service Companies 906.0   Net interest expense (net of tax) 39.4
Corporate and unallocated items 10.0
Geographic ($m) Worldwide 8,343.2

BALANCE SHEETS (A$'M)	1990	1991	1992	1993	1994 Half Year
Total Current Assets	5,025.1	4,784.7	4,687.1	4,940.5	
Non Current Assets					
Receivables	618.4	902.7	936.8	984.5	
Investments	1,454.9	1,703.2	1,354.3	2,765.1	
Inventories	121.5	108.9	101.9	112.1	
Property, plant & equipment	13,310.8	13,849.9	15,422.0	16,196.9	
Intangibles	207.8	276.0	330.7	353.7	
Other	296.6	528.1	754.8	878.9	
Total Non Current Assets	16,010.0	17,368.8	18,900.5	21,291.2	
TOTAL ASSETS	21,035.1	22,153.5	23,587.6	26,231.7	
Total Current Liabilities	4,115.9	4,985.7	6,085.2	5,423.3	
Non Current Liabilities					
Creditors & borrowin.gs	7,408.0	6,610.5	5,848.7	6,304.8	
Provisions	2,898.0	2,947.5	3,247.3	3,260.0	
Tot Non Current Liabilities	10,306.0	9,558.0	9,096.0	9,564.8	
TOTAL LIABILITIES	14,421.9	14,543.7	15,181.2	14,988.1	
NET ASSETS	6,613.2	7,609.8	8,406.4	11,243.6	
Shareholders' Equity					
Share capital	5,433.9	6,662.4	7,525.5	1,646.7	
Reserves	–	–	–	3,429.7	
Retained profits	–	–	–	5,916.8	
Minority interests	1,179.2	947.4	880.9	250.4	
TOT S'HOLDERS' EQ'TY	6,613.2	7,609.8	8,406.4	11,243.6	

DIRECTORY

Head Office and Registered Address 48th Floor, BHP Tower, 600 Bourke Street, Melbourne VIC 3000. Ph (03) 609 3333 Fax (03) 609 3015. **Principal Share Registry** 40th Floor, BHP Tower, 600 Bourke Street, Melbourne VIC 3000. Phone (03) 609 3333 Fax (03) 810 8526.

Directors BT Loton AC (Chairman,) JB Prescott (MD & CEO), JB Reid AO, JB Gough AO OBE, DW Rogers, Sir Eric Neal AC CVO, GE Heeley, PJ Willcox, DJ Asimus AO, JK Ellis, RJ McNeilly. **Senior Management** JB Prescott (MD & CEO), GE Heeley (Exec GM Finance), JE Lewis (Exec GM Corporate Planning and Administration), JK Ellis (Exec GM & CEO Minerals), PJ Willcox (Exec GM & CEO Petroleum), RJ McNeilly (Exec GM & CEO Steel), GW McGregor (Exec GM & CEO Service Companies). **Company Secretary** TJ Knott
Auditors Arthur Andersen & Co
Bankers Not given
Solicitors Not given

PROFIT & LOSS ACCOUNTS

	1990	1991	1992	1993	1994
Total Revenue	14,019.7	16,836.3	14,960.6	16,680.4	8,118.6
Operating profit incl abnorms	1,625.5	1,937.3	1,327.5	1,889.7	1,093.0
Income tax (credit)	582.3	575.9	738.7	596.0	376.7
Minority interest	87.8	90.5	74.0	99.3	76.3
Extraordinary profit (loss)	–	–	–	–	–
Attributable Profit	955.4	1,270.9	514.8	1,194.4	640.0
Dividends	499.6	570.9	465.5	484.5	21c/sh

STATISTICS ASX Research

	1990	1991	1992	1993	1994
EPS Historical (c)	75.84	107.32	41.81	92.29	48.10
Adjusted (c)	75.84	107.32	41.61	92.29	48.10
INTERIM DIV (c)	17.50	19.50	19.50	19.50	21.00
FRANKING (%)	100	100	100	100	100
FINAL DIV (c)	19.00	21.00	21.00	21.00	
FRANKING (%)	100	100	100	100	
NTA Historical ($)	5.03	5.36	5.71	6.47	
Adjusted ($)	5.03	5.36	5.71	6.47	
PRICE High ($)	11.60	15.60	14.64	17.96	
Low ($)	8.72	9.30	10.18	12.58	

CAPITAL STRUCTURE

31 May 1993:   1,646.5 ord shares of $1 fp.   9.5m ord shares of $1 pd to 1c. 2.0m ord shares of $1 pd to 5c.

SHAREHOLDER INFORMATION as at 4 August 1993

Top 20	m	%		m	%
Beswick Group	322.6	19.3	ANZ Nominees	94.4	5.7
AMP Society	78.2	4.7	National Nominees	58.2	3.5
Westpac Custodian Noms	47.4	2.8	State Authorities Super	38.7	2.3
National Mutual Group	28.8	1.7	Pendal Nominees	27.5	1.6
Qld Investment Corp	25.0	1.5	Chase Manhattan Noms	24.5	1.5
Perpetual Trustee Aust	24.4	1.5	MLC Life	23.6	1.4
CBA Nominees	17.0	1.0	Citicorp Nominees	14.4	0.9
Transport Accident Comm	11.3	0.7	Permanent Trustee Co	10.5	0.6
Commonwealth Super	10.5	0.6	Prudential Assurance	9.2	0.6
Mitsubishi Development	8.6	0.5	Colonial Mutual Group	8.4	0.5

Substantial Beswick Group 327.5m
Number of Shareholders 215,000

Last AGM: 29/09/93   **Divs payable (approx):** November and May/June

The Australian Financial Review Shareholder   Copyright Stafford McWilliams Pty Ltd 1994

TABLE B: RATES OF RETURN
(*Superfunds* Magazine)

(*% per annum*)

Period Covered	Typical Fund Performance	AWE	CPI	Real Rate of Return
5 Years Ended: at 30th June				
1977	3.9	15.3	12.4	−9.9
1978	6.9	15.5	13.2	−7.4
1979	13.2	13.8	12.2	−0.5
1980	18.7	10.8	10.9	7.1
1981	17.8	10.7	10.2	6.4
1982	15.5	11.1	9.5	4.0
1983	17.6	11.4	9.9	5.6
1984	17.7	11.3	9.7	5.8
1985	14.8	10.7	8.5	3.7
1986	17.6	9.2	8.3	7.7
1987	24.9	7.7	8.1	16.0
1988	19.5	6.6	7.2	12.1
1989	18.6	6.6	7.3	11.3
1990	16.5	6.7	8.1	9.2
1991	12.2	6.6	7.5	5.3
1992	8.4	5.8	5.9	2.5
1993	10.5	5.1	4.7	5.1
10 Years Ended: at 30th June				
1977	8.5	11.9	8.2	−3.0
1978	6.3	12.3	8.8	−5.3
1979	6.8	12.4	9.4	−5.0
1980	10.5	12.5	10.1	−1.8
1981	12.0	12.7	10.6	−0.6
1982	9.6	13.2	11.0	−3.2
1983	12.2	13.4	11.5	−1.1
1984	15.4	12.5	10.9	2.6
1985	16.7	10.7	9.7	5.4
1986	17.7	9.9	9.2	7.1
1987	20.1	9.4	8.8	9.8
1988	18.5	9.0	8.6	8.7

	TABLE B CONTINUED			
Period Covered	Typical Fund Performance	AWE	CPI	Real Rate of Return
1989	18.1	8.9	8.5	8.4
1990	15.7	8.7	8.3	6.4
1991	14.9	7.9	7.9	6.5
1992	16.4	6.8	7.0	9.0
1993	14.9	5.9	6.0	8.5
15 Years Ended: at 30th June				
1977	8.0	9.7	6.2	-1.5
1978	8.2	10.2	6.8	-1.8
1979	8.3	10.4	7.3	-1.9
1980	11.3	10.5	7.7	0.7
1981	11.8	11.1	8.1	0.6
1982	10.8	11.6	8.7	-0.7
1983	10.0	12.0	9.2	-1.8
1984	10.3	12.0	9.5	-1.5
1985	11.9	11.9	9.6	0.0
1986	13.8	11.6	9.8	2.0
1987	14.5	11.3	10.0	2.0
1988	14.5	11.1	10.1	3.1
1989	16.5	10.5	9.7	5.4
1990	16.7	9.4	9.1	6.7
1991	15.9	8.8	8.6	6.5
1992	16.1	8.2	7.8	7.3
1993	15.8	9.7	7.3	7.5
20 Years Ended: at 30th June				
1982	9.8	10.0	7.0	-0.2
1983	10.5	10.5	7.6	0.0
1984	10.5	10.6	7.9	-0.1
1985	12.1	10.6	7.9	1.4
1986	13.3	10.6	8.2	2.4
1987	14.2	10.6	8.5	3.3
1988	12.3	10.6	8.7	1.5
1989	12.3	10.6	9.9	1.5
1990	13.0	10.6	9.2	2.2
1991	13.4	10.3	9.2	2.8
1992	12.9	9.9	9.0	2.7
1993	13.5	9.6	8.7	3.6

	TABLE B CONTINUED			
Period Covered	Typical Fund Performance	AWE	CPI	Real Rate of Return
25 Years Ended: at 30th June				
1987	12.7	9.6	7.2	2.8
1988	12.3	9.7	7.5	2.4
1989	12.1	9.8	7.8	2.1
1990	13.0	9.8	7.9	2.9
1991	13.0	9.8	8.0	2.9
1992	13.0	9.7	8.0	3.0
1993	11.9	9.5	7.9	2.2
30 Year Ended: at 30th June				
1992	11.9	8.9	7.0	2.8
1993	12.0	8.9	7.0	2.8

How the figures were calculated

The figures for typical fund performance have been derived where possible from the average rates of return of funds participating in actuarial surveys.

Prior to 1 July 1970, the figures were drawn from model fund calculations. These used individual sector performance figures obtained from averaging the investment return of the appropriate units in the No 2 Statutory Funds of the AMP Society and National Mutual, whilst for some early years figures were obtained from Stock Exchange indices and Commonwealth Bond yields. The model fund calculations assumed the proportions of 30% Government Securities (G), 15% Other fixed interest (O), 55% Shares (S) where statistics were available and 40% G, 60% S where statistics were available only for G and S.

From 1970 to 1989 the figures were the average rates of returns of funds participating in the IMS survey (1970 to 1987) and the TPF&C survey (1987 to 1989). From 1 July

1989 onwards the figure are derived form the Asset-weighted Average of the TPF&C Superannuation Pooled Funds Survey.

AWE is average weekly total earnings for males as published by the Australian Bureau of Statistics.

CPI is the Consumer Price Index eight capitals figure for All Groups published by the Australian Bureau of Statistics.

Real Rate of Return is equal to the ratio of the typical fund performance return to the rate of increase in AWE. For example, if the typical fund performance for a period is 8% and the AWE for the same period is 7%, the real rate of return is: 1.08 divided by 1.07 minus one equals 0.93%.

TABLE C: DECLINE IN THE PURCHASING POWER OF THE
DOLLAR
(J.B. Were & Son)

As at 30th June	Consumer Price Index (Weighted Average of 6 State Capitals) 1980-81 = 100*	Dollar Value		
		1960 = 100	1970 = 100	1980 = 100
1960	13.7	100.0		
1961	14.2	96.9		
1962	14.1	97.5		
1963	14.1	97.2		
1964	14.4	95.5		
1965	15.0	91.7		
1966	15.5	88.8		
1967	15.9	86.3		
1968	16.4	83.8		
1969	16.9	81.5		
1970	17.5	78.5	100.0	
1971	18.4	74.5	94.9	
1972	19.6	70.2	89.3	
1973	21.2	64.8	82.6	
1974	24.2	56.7	72.2	
1975	28.4	48.5	61.7	
1976	31.8	43.2	54.9	
1977	36.1	38.0	48.4	
1978	39.0	35.3	44.9	
1979	42.4	32.4	41.3	
1980	47.0	29.3	37.3	100.0
1981	51.1	26.9	34.2	91.9
1982	56.6	24.3	30.9	83.0
1983	62.9	21.8	27.8	74.6
1984	65.3	21.0	26.8	71.9
1985	69.7	19.7	25.1	67.3
1986	75.6	18.2	23.1	62.1
1987	82.6	16.6	21.2	56.8
1988	88.5	15.5	19.8	53.1
1989	95.2	14.4	18.4	49.3
1990	102.5	13.4	17.1	45.8
1991	106.0	13.0	16.5	44.3
1992	107.3	12.8	16.3	43.8
1993	109.3	12.6	16.0	43.0

* The Australian Bureau of Statistics is using the *average* of
the 4 quarterly indices as the statistical base. In the March
1987 quarter it ceased publication of the 'Weighted Average of
6 State Capitals' series. We continued the above by using its
'W.A. of 8 Capital Cities' series (the deviation is negligible)

TABLE D: SHARES VS DEBENTURES
(J.B. Were & Son)

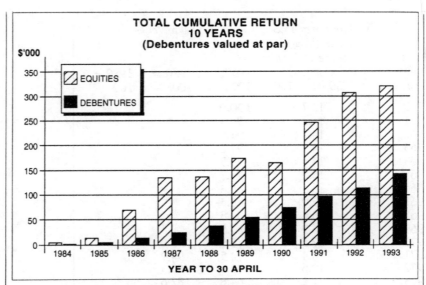

Investment of $200,000 Over Ten Years

	CUMULATIVE INCOME	CAPITAL GAIN	TOTAL GAIN
Shares	$ 81,096	$239,766	$320,862
Debentures	$147,830	$ 32,484	$180,314

■ For many years we have maintained this survey based on the hypothetical investment of $20,000 annually into both ordinary shares and debentures.

The investment has been timed at 30 April in each year. In the case of the equities when there has been a cash share issue, the rights accruing on the holding have been sold and old shares purchased so that any shareholder benefit from the issue has been accounted for without the injection of any additional funds.

■ The ordinary shares selected for the annual investment have been in the following companies:

> Brambles Industries Limited
> The Broken Hill Proprietary Company Limited
> Coca-Cola Amatil Limited
> Coles Myer Ltd
> CSR Limited
> Foster's Brewing Group Limited
> The News Corporation Limited
> North Broken Hill Peko Limited
> Pacific Dunlop Limited
> Westpac Banking Corporation

TABLE E: TAX SHELTERING FROM DIVIDEND IMPUTATION
1994/95
(ANZ McCaughan/Coopers & Lybrand)

Fully Franked Dividend* $	Max. Level of Other Income Earned Tax Free $	Tax (and Medicare) Payable after Imputation Credit $	Tax Saved on Other Income** $	Net Tax Saving (Cost) $
1,000	6,957.38	0.00	311.48	311.48
2,000	8,514.75	0.00	622.95	622.95
3,000	10,072.13	209.86	934.43	865.57
4,000	11,629.51	254.62	1,245.90	1,154.10
5,000	12,905.40	295.43	1,501.08	1,386.33
6,000	13,146.48	321.76	1,549.30	1,411.59
7,000	13,387.56	348.08	1,597.51	1,436.86
8,000	13,628.64	374.41	1,645.73	1,462.12
9,000	13,869.72	400.73	1,693.94	1,487.39
10,000	14,110.80	427.06	1,742.16	1,512.65
11,000	14,351.88	453.39	1,790.38	1,537.92
12,000	14,592.96	479.71	1,838.59	1,563.18
13,000	14,834.04	506.04	1,886.81	1,588.45
14,000	15,069.69	532.29	1,933.94	1,612.63
15,000	14,917.19	553.10	1,903.44	1,559.18
16,000	14,764.70	573.92	1,872.94	1,505.73
17,000	14,612.20	594.73	1,842.44	1,452.28
18,000	14,459.70	615.55	1,811.94	1,398.83
19,000	14,307.21	636.37	1,781.44	1,345.38
20,000	14,154.71	657.18	1,750.94	1,291.93
21,000	14,002.21	678.00	1,720.44	1,238.48
22,000	13,849.71	698.81	1,689.94	1,185.02
23,000	13,577.89	717.96	1,635.58	1,107.71
24,000	13,298.85	737.00	1,579.77	1,028.95
25,000	13,019.81	756.05	1,523.96	950.19
26,000	12,740.77	775.09	1,468.15	871.43
27,000	12,461.74	794.14	1,412.35	792.68
28,000	12,182.70	813.18	1,356.54	713.92
29,000	11,903.66	832.23	1,300.73	635.16
30,000	11,624.63	851.27	1,244.93	556.40
31,000	11,345.59	870.31	1,189.12	477.64
32,000	11,066.55	889.36	1,133.31	398.88
33,000	10,787.51	908.40	1,077.50	320.13
34,000	10,508.48	927.45	1,021.70	241.37
35,000	10,229.44	946.49	965.89	162.61
36,000	9,950.40	965.54	910.08	83.85
37,000	9,671.36	984.58	854.27	5.09
38,000	9,392.33	1,003.62	798.47	(73.67)
39,000	9,113.29	1,022.67	742.66	(152.42)

TABLE E: CONTINUED

Fully Franked Dividend* $	Max. Level of Other Income Earned Tax Free $	Tax (and Medicare) Payable after Imputation Credit $	Tax Saved on Other Income** $	Net Tax Saving (Cost) $
40,000	8,834.25	1,041.71	686.85	(231.18)
41,000	8,555.21	1,060.76	631.04	(309.94)
42,000	8,276.18	1,079.80	575.24	(388.70)
43,000	7,997.14	1,098.85	519.43	(467.46)
44,000	7,718.10	1,117.89	463.62	(546.22)
45,000	7,439.07	1,136.93	407.81	(624.97)
46,000	7,160.03	1,155.98	352.01	(703.73)
47,000	6,880.99	1,175.02	296.20	(782.49)
48,000	6,601.95	1,194.07	240.39	(861.25)
49,000	6,322.92	1,213.11	184.58	(940.01)
50,000	6,403.88	1,232.16	128.78	(1,018.77)
51,000	5,764.84	1,251.20	72.97	(1,097.52)
52,000	5,485.80	1,270.24	17.16	(1,176.28)
53,000	5,206.77	1,289.29	0.00	(1,216.39)
54,000	4,927.73	1,308.33	0.00	(1,239.34)
55,000	4,648.69	1,327.38	0.00	(1,262.30)
56,000	4,369.65	1,346.42	0.00	(1,285.25)
57,000	4,090.62	1,365.47	0.00	(1,308.20)
58,000	3,811.58	1,384.51	0.00	(1,331.15)
59,000	3,532.54	1,403.55	0.00	(1,354.10)
60,000	3,253.51	1,422.60	0.00	(1,377.05)
61,000	2,974.47	1,441.64	0.00	(1,400.00)
62,000	2,695.43	1,460.69	0.00	(1,422.95)
63,000	2,416.39	1,479.73	0.00	(1,445.90)
64,000	2,137.36	1,498.78	0.00	(1,468.85)
65,000	1,858.32	1,517.82	0.00	(1,491.80)
66,000	1,579.28	1,536.86	0.00	(1,514.75)
67,000	1,300.24	1,555.91	0.00	(1,537.70)
68,000	1,021.21	1,574.95	0.00	(1,560.66)
69,000	742.17	1,594.00	0.00	(1,583.61)
70,000	463.13	1,613.04	0.00	(1,606.56)
71,000	184.09	1,632.09	0.00	(1,629.51)
72,000	0.00	1,697.08	0.00	(1,652.46)

* Assumes dividend is franked with 39% tax credits. Some companies may only be able to pass on 33% tax credits.
** Assumes other income is the 'bottom slice' of taxable income.

Other assumptions:

1. The table applies to individuals only, and does not apply to non-residents, or residents aged under 18 years, at year end.
2. The table ignores any other rebates or tax credits, or special bases of assessment (such as averaging) to which a taxpayer may be entitled.
3. The Medicare levy calculations assume that the taxpayer is single, hence the lower threshold has been used.

TABLE F: INCOME TAX SCALE
YEAR TO 30 JUNE 1995
AUSTRALIAN RESIDENT INDIVIDUALS

Taxable Income thresholds	% tax
0–$5400	–
$5401–20,700	20
$20,701–38,000	34
$38,001–50,000	43
Over $50,000	47

Plus Medicare levy of 1.4%

TABLE G: INVESTOR RETURN—TEN YEARS
(Statex Service of the ASX)
$1000 INVESTED–31 DECEMBER 1983 TO 31 DECEMBER 1993

	Current Value ($)	Compound Return (%)
Lemarne	75,012.11	54.00
BTR Nylex	64,595.87	51.71
Sons of Gwalia	37,759.88	43.78
Samantha	36,768.00	43.40
North Flinders	34,803.55	42.61
Normandy Poseidon	24,645.17	37.78
Delta Gold	22,778.37	36.69
Hancock & Gore	19,184.10	34.37
Danks Holdings	18,580.93	33.94
Westfield Holdings	18,401.79	33.81
Resolute	17,671.76	33.27
News Corporation	17,254.01	32.95
Sunraysia	17,117.82	32.84
Allgas	16,990.87	32.75
Perpetual T. Tas	16,463.61	32.33
Coca Cola Amatil	15,673.08	31.68
Mildara Blass	14,435.30	30.60
Scott	14,086.85	30.28
Posgold	14,031.75	30.23
Queensland Metals	13,330.96	29.56
F.H. Faulding	13,153.05	29.39
Hills Industries	12,555.33	28.79
Jeffries	12,414.11	28.64
QBE Insurance	12,118.66	28.34
Email	12,097.57	28.31
Niugini Mining	11,954.59	28.16
Reece Australia	11,789.42	27.98
Arnotts	10,882.03	26.96
Herald	10,473.60	26.48
G.M. Aust	10,282.01	26.24
Bunnings	10,224.31	26.17
Gibson's	10,220.41	26.17
Cudgen	10,047.37	25.95
Westralian Forests	9,449.43	25.18
Wattyl	9,209.48	24.86
Sylvastate	9,190.82	24.83
Linden & Conway	9,077.01	24.68
St Barbara	8,993.63	24.56
National Aust Bank	8,640.76	24.07

INDEX